Sepia-Toned Archives

Bob Wilkinson

SEPIA-TONED ARCHIVES

Second Edition

Published 2023
Printed in the United States of America
Paperback ISBN: 978-0-9970123-5-4
Hardback ISBN: 978-0-9970123-6-1
E-book ISBN: 978-0-9970123-8-5

Library of Congress Cataloging-in-Publication Data

Editor/Publisher: Willy Wilkinson
Scanner Extraordinaire: Su-Lin Wilkinson
Cover art by Bob Wilkinson
Cover by Dolce Vita Design

Hapa Papa Press
PO Box 27401
Oakland, CA 94602
www.willywilkinson.com

Sepia-Toned Archives

Bob Wilkinson

HPP

Hapa Papa Press

SEPIA-TONED ARCHIVES

Table of Contents

Hitchhiker's Guide For The Octogenarian

Can't remember people's names?
Or the rules of card games?
Just wisely smile while you tell 'em,
Its age's toll on the cerebellum.

You may be proud of your youthful stance
Or rumba steps and vigorous tap dance;
But you may soon discover that railings
Can prevent unchoreographed downstairs sailings.

Avoid uncomfortable consternation
By stopping at the next gas station;
Besides knees becoming a little creaky
Your plumbing may also get a tad leaky.

While finding teen's styles as uncouth
You can indulge in stories of your youth.

But though others may politely insist,
From giving advice you should desist.
For nuggets of wisdom they can be buyers
Of your soon-to-be published memoirs.

If questions on Jeopardy leave you without voice
Just say that you'd be champ with multiple choice.

If you don't know an iPod from a tripod,
And think Twitter is from a feathered critter,
You may yet have the last laugh
Just ask *them* about carbon paper or mimeograph.

Brush up on all the new meds before getting together
The stuff of eighties talk--more common than the weather.

BOB WILKINSON

Finally, beware of compliments so glib from the tongue
Saying "My, you look so young!"
When all is said,
They're just surprised you're not yet dead.

Feb. 2011

A Shoebox View of Life

Boxed In

One way to keep a family's expenses within the confines of a tight budget is the method devised by my mother in the 1930's. It allowed for very few digressions from the amounts set aside at the beginning of each month's planning.

In our family of five, our Central Bank was a cardboard shoebox in my parents' bedroom in which were kept a series of envelopes. Each envelope contained the monthly budgeted amounts of cash, in dollar bills and change, for each anticipated household expense. Groceries, Pacific Gas and Electric (PG&E), gasoline, haircuts— all were represented there in their marked envelopes available only for those designated needs. When the iceman brought a block of ice balanced on his shoulder and heaved it into the icebox, my mother went to the shoebox, and he was paid by cash withdrawn from the envelope marked "ICE." My father's train and lunch money came from their own packets; the milk bill was paid in the same way.

The envelopes at one time must have been clean, fresh, and unwrinkled; my recollection was that they were crumpled and soiled with the doughy fingers of someone who may have been interrupted while baking bread, or smudged by hands that had just been digging in the garden. My mother was the envelope exchequer, doling out just the necessary amount from only the proper envelope.

But what to do when an emergency arose such as car repair or a medical emergency? That occurred, for example, when I broke my wrist, necessitating an unusual trip to the family doctor, something that was undertaken only in dire emergencies. There was no envelope marked "broken bones," so paying the bill would require a careful analysis, assessing the risks of raiding from some other envelope. What tradesman or what company can be put off until next month? Which had been let slide most recently and therefore was probably less tolerant of another backsliding? Could the clothing envelope be dipped into and the needed jacket or sweater postponed, or the shoes repaired one more time instead of being replaced?

For my mother, this was not always an easy decision, but often accompanied with sighing, much sturm and drang, so that I and my sisters were not sheltered from the tension occasioned by the emergency, and therefore became sensitive to the financial and emotional consequences of unbudgeted expenses. The tensions could be replaced by smiles and laughter, however, if a bill came in lower than anticipated, or there was a small unexpected gift of money from a relative, as sometimes happened.

Now, when we embarked on our project to raise chickens, partly to relieve the pressure on the shoe box, and later also because of wartime meat rationing, a greater level of complexity was introduced into the task of assigning money to envelopes, the grocery envelopes for instance. We discovered that chickens could not always be relied upon to carry out their responsibilities, and on time. They could sicken and die of unknown causes. Rats could, and did, create havoc among the flocks and eggs. The weather had some impacts on their egg-laying discipline, so the risks of life as farmers came to be better appreciated by us amateurs. Maybe there was a reason for farm loans.

But the envelope system, although strained, persisted. One result was that we children came to incorporate into our very DNA the lessons contained in that shoe box, lessons that were very useful in surviving earlier, more economically stringent days. Thriftiness, Benjamin Franklin-like frugality, delayed gratification—it all seemed consistent with a shoebox approach to life. It is open to question, however, to what extent they remained so applicable as times got better for us in adult life. A shoebox view of life required too much discipline, a too cramped, boxed-in lifestyle in an environment of checking accounts and easy credit cards.

Ordinary Life During The Depression, 1930 -1940

Some of my earliest memories of the Depression years were school-related. For example, when I was in first or second grade, I remember walking into the schoolgrounds in Riverside one morning and finding a wooden box full of oranges lying beside the entrance, apparently a generous gift from someone in the community to local schoolchildren. I took one. Only looking back does it seem like a Depression-era memory—a time when an anonymous gift of oranges or any food would seem unheard of, even though we lived in the citrus-growing area.

My sister Martha recalls the fig tree that, at that time, grew in our Riverside backyard, which fortunately also provided us with its fruit.

Another memory is associated with my classroom in Alameda, probably in 1933, which would have been my first or second grade class. Our teacher halted whatever she was teaching, standing aside, as though by prior arrangement. A boy, obviously from an upper grade, came into the room, walked to the blackboard, and using the broad side of a piece of chalk, drew an eagle with outspread wings. The symbol I was to understand later was of one of recently elected President Franklin Delano Roosevelt (FDR)'s programs to deal with the Depression. I did not understand the implications of the symbol, which had become almost a patriotic one, but my parents seemed to when I recounted the story. It was only in later years that I came to realize its significance as the Blue Eagle, the political emblem of the National Recovery Act, or NRA. But it is often surprising to me that the image has survived in my memory all this time, and the only memory I have of the Alameda school.

The move from Riverside to Alameda was because of my father getting a job with the Internal Revenue Service in San Francisco. I understood that the job came to him through the influence of a relative whose name I don't recall. It provided the first dependable source of income for the family. He worked six days a week, commuting by train (Sacramento Northern) to the ferry terminal, and then across the bay to San Francisco.

I had heard that Mother in earlier times had to leave Dad and return home to Salt Lake with me to live with her parents when times had gotten too difficult financially for them, Dad not having a job, in particular, or not being paid for his work because the company went bankrupt. Relatives paid the expense of the trip back to Utah.

When we moved to a rented house in the Montclair District in the Oakland hills in the 1930's, we settled into a house without the accoutrements associated now with proper housing. It must have been an inexpensive relocation because we lacked a water heater. To have a warm bath we had to heat pots of water on the stove and carry them into the bathroom. A wringer washer, common in those days, was the centerpiece of every Saturday's tasks, leading sometimes to us children getting our arms painfully caught in the wringer.

Refrigeration was by ice of course, usual in those days, the ice man delivering the seventy-five pound block of ice on his shoulder down from the street to the kitchen ice chest. While he was thus occupied, we children would raid the canvas-covered back of the ice truck, carrying off in triumph whatever shards of ice we could scrounge before he returned to the truck.

Also, there was no garbage collection in our neighborhood, so every two or three weeks my father and I would dig a hole for the accumulated rubbish. I had the job of smashing the cans smaller with the head of an axe to reduce the overall volume of garbage, often resulting in the squirting out of the can's remaining smelly contents onto me or my father.

No regular sewage system existed either. The house had a septic tank with drainage in the backyard, sometimes requiring a day of digging up to remove tree roots blocking it.

SEPIA-TONED ARCHIVES

We didn't have toys that we think little of purchasing now, but what we did have was the remains of an old covered wagon in the backyard which sparked much imaginative play. The canvas top was long gone, but the wooden wagon box and two or three of the wheels remained. The front part of the wagon could be moved from side to side, as though being turned by the oxen still hitched to it. It afforded opportunity for pioneer play, recreating the journey across the plains taken by our mother's ancestors en route to Utah. We fended off thundering herds of buffalo, hostile Indians, and foiled robbers, with the help of my trusty cap pistol.

Also, there was the sparsely inhabited, tree-covered neighborhood in which to wander. One of my favorite pastimes was to throw rocks—at trees, dogs, almost anything, sometimes getting me into trouble, as when once a rock I threw missed its target and struck a car just rounding the curve ahead. As it passed by me, the looks I got from the passengers and driver were a bit hostile.

I remember hiking up to the old tunnel on Grizzly Peak Blvd. that had been replaced by construction of the Caldecott Tunnel. The old tunnel was still open, but was seldom used. It leaked water onto the roadway and was supported only by wooden construction. It was scarcely lit by thinly-spaced bare light bulbs, which I usually took aim at with a rock. Eventually, that tunnel was boarded up and closed off to traffic.

Another pastime was the throwing of spears at one another, obtained from pulling four- or five-foot long woody stalks of a sturdy weed from the marshy ground about half a mile away. I marvel that no eyes were put out, that I know of, by this hazardous combat.

I used packed pine needles to build forts among the pines that were common in our neighborhood in those days—probably burned out though by recent fires—and indulged in fantasies of warfare, sometimes recruiting my sisters as warriors, sometimes to their confusion of why they should hurt our neighboring children if they approached with no harmful intent.

BOB WILKINSON

We walked to our school in Montclair, one and a half miles away. The initial part was by dirt trail down the eucalyptus-covered hillside to the road below. School consisted of six portables, each heated with a pot-bellied, coal-burning stove. The desks had an inkwell hole in the upper left corner; each student had to supply their own ink, pen, and blotter.

An auditorium was on the grounds, about a hundred yards downhill, not far from the Carnegie-funded library. Portables had recently replaced the two-story brick structure, closed because of new state school regulations following an earthquake. The playground displayed very little that could be used for recreation. Therefore, we relied on what we could bring in our pockets, like marbles which were carried, often in an old Bull Durham tobacco sack, which would be pulled out of the pocket at recess. A fish-shaped or round circle would be drawn in the dirt and some marbles placed within it. A marble shooter would be used to try to knock as many marbles as possible out of the ring, which the shooter owner could then keep. There probably were other rules pertaining to the game. Also, a game we played was to see who could land their marble closest to the building; the winner got the opponents' marbles.

Another game was played at recess with the tops of milk bottles. The point was to drop your top onto the one just dropped by your opponent. If yours covered your opponent's top completely, both tops were yours. Mother didn't like my tendency to take the tops off milk bottles before the bottles were used.

One game required ten cents for purchasing the essentials, which were balsa wood gliders that we would sail into the air, trying to hit other gliders. It often meant retrieving the gliders from the schoolroom roof.

We boys were all apt to carry other things in our pockets. They included baseball cards, although no major league team existed in our area. Babe Ruth, Lou Gehrig, or other prominent player cards were

17

worth more than some of those of the lesser-known players. They came with bubble gum attached to the reverse side. They were purchased from the local barber, who had a candy counter next to the barber chair, with him interrupting his sales occasionally to cut hair.

Other pocket items included rubber bands with which to launch wads of paper as projectiles (my sisters often being the long-suffering victims) and a pocket knife. When not in school, I also carried a cap pistol obtained by sending in six box tops from Wheaties, plus twenty-five cents. Although the holster was not leather, but probably cheap cardboard, I felt sure I was the well-equipped nemesis of any outlaw on the range.

One of the foods I remember clearly, although not fondly, was margarine, a white substance that replaced the more expensive butter. It could be given a yellow color by stirring in a small package of artificial coloring, using a sturdy wooden spoon with the partially warmed-up margarine in a large bowl, then to be spread on bread or toast.

The thrill that comes once in a lifetime, or anyway by age nine, occurred when I purchased for five cents (the going rate at that time) a cone of ice cream at a shop, and as I left the shop, felt something metallic against my tongue as I licked the cone. With further licking, it turned out to be the nickel I had paid the shop girl who had apparently dropped it into the cone while scooping the ice cream. It was my weekly allowance. I kept on walking, amazed at my good fortune, instead of returning the nickel to the shop.

At about twelve or so, I became fascinated by ships, learning all the names of sails used in the days of sailing ships. I once gave a verbal report in class about the sails, naming the various kinds, like the top sail, the foresail, etc. The teacher Mrs. Bachelor's only comment afterward was that she was struck by one name I listed—the spanker.

I soon began making small model wooden ships, usually navy ships, which I played with as though they were a real armada. It is uncertain whether it had anything to do with my later-in-life venture into wood sculpture.

As for entertainment, we seldom saw any movies, but I will always remember the Walt Disney movie *Snow White and The Seven Dwarfs.* I am unsure under what auspices we saw it. Was it at school, or was it in a theater?

I had some favorite radio programs which could cause me to hurry home from school to listen to. Ones that I can remember were *The Lone Ranger* and *Jack Armstrong, the All American Boy.* I also recall my father and I listening to the heavyweight boxing matches, usually including Joe Louis who once fought against the German Max Schmelling. My mother was disgusted with our listening to that kind of physical fighting.

Games were often played by our family, since TV was far into the future. One in particular was the card game "Authors," by which I learned the names of American and English writers, which may have been Mother's unexpressed intent. Authors I came to know this way included Edgar Allen Poe, Ralph Waldo Emerson, Arthur Conan Doyle, and Mark Twain.

Songs from the Depression era that I can recall included "Brother Can You Spare a Dime" (Rudy Vallee), "Happy Days are Here Again," and "On the Sunny Side of the Street" (Frank Sinatra). Also, Woody Guthrie sang "I Ain't Got No Home."

Favorite comic strips for me date from about 1940 when the economy began to ease, as I don't think our family could afford to take a newspaper when the Depression was at its worst. My favorites were The Katzenjammer Kids (the choice of which my mother couldn't tolerate), Li'l Orphan Annie, Dick Tracy, Li'l Abner, and Tarzan.

SEPIA-TONED ARCHIVES

The World's Fair on Treasure Island opened in early 1939, partly in celebration of the completion of both the Golden Gate and the Bay Bridges. We attended at least twice to view the various exhibits, one of which I think had a preview of the earliest version of television. What I remember best was not the exhibitions, but the souvenir aluminum disks with the symbols of the fair imprinted on them. I had to stand in a long line to receive one, which I did over and over. It may have been the effect of the Depression on me, to obtain something free, although of no practical value, but they looked almost like coins. Also, I remember the slow speed of Pan American float planes that landed and took off from the lagoon at Treasure Island, close to Yerba Buena Island.

Although I was generally insulated from the stress of the expense of daily living, we knew that Mother had her way of managing the costs of everything by the use of the shoebox. The recent failure of most of the banks in the country may have been one of the reasons for the envelope system.

To earn some spending money, I had a magazine route, delivering weekly magazines, and having to collect ten cents or whatever the cost was, each week. Probably the reason for a cash economy was that people could not afford to pay an annual subscription, but could manage to put a dime or fifteen cents together once a week. I graduated later to carrying the twice weekly shopping news, toting heavily-laden canvas pouches hanging front and back from my shoulders, up and down the hills for several hours. To save time and energy, I would fold the shopping news and toss it in the direction of the front doors of houses. I remember one time the paper landed mistakenly on the outdoor coffee table where a family was gathered for breakfast. I think coffee was liberally sprayed in the air and the cups knocked off the table; I quickly ducked out of sight.

I don't remember anything about my clothing except for shoes. If our shoes developed holes in their soles, the remedy was not to buy new ones, but to purchase, for a few cents, a kit for re-soling. It consisted of new soles, and a right-angle-shaped metal strip with an abrasive surface, which was used to roughen the surface of both the old and the new soles, and a tube of glue. The procedure was to apply the adhesive after roughening the surfaces, apply the new sole, and apply pressure to hold the new sole to the old shoe. Fine, but within a few hours of use, the sole would loosen and flap uncomfortably whenever a step was taken. I called them "Alligator" shoes because of the open jaws effect upon taking a step. To me, it was a very unwelcome method of saving.

As the Depression began to ebb, we took some vacation camping trips to Big Basin in the coastal Redwoods. Before the Bay Bridge was built, the journey involved taking a ferry from Oakland to San Francisco, which was a kind of thrill to me. While the car was parked in the boat, I would explore its two levels, including the snack shop, and the glimpse of some of the boat's mechanism. When we approached the ferry slip in San Francisco, I would watch with interest the two men who dropped the automobile gangplank, accompanied by the loud rattle of supporting chains, then the directing of motorists to leave, a few at a time from first the port side, then the starboard side of the boat.

Then it was time for us to scurry back to our car in time for us to leave. Eventually, while traveling across the Bay, we were able to glimpse the early stages of construction of the Bay Bridge. The concrete piers were funded by the Works Progress Administration (WPA). While impressive as the trip was to us kids, it was an everyday experience for my father who worked in San Francisco six days a week.

Then, straight up Market Street, through the agricultural fields that are now Daly City, and onto Skyline Boulevard to Big Basin, roughly between San Jose and Santa Cruz. There was no Highway 101 in those days, of course.

Big Basin, the first state park in California, was a glorious vacation trip for us. A short path took one around the individually-named ancient redwoods. There were hiking trails, wading in the creek, and

21

above all, the campfire gatherings in the evenings when we sat on redwood logs in a semicircle around a blazing fire, singing songs led by a young ranger. Songs like "Push the damper in, push the damper out, and the smoke goes up the chimney just the same," and "John Jacob Jingleheimer Schmidt--that's my name too." "Do your ears hang low, do they wobble to and fro?" were some of the favorites.

There was a small museum which told the history of the area, including the interesting fact to me that Grizzly bears once were a danger to people in the vicinity.

Sadly, one of the fires in recent years razed Big Basin.

Once or twice, we went by ferry from near Richmond to Sausalito to visit Mother's brother Sterling and his family—his wife Meda, and two boys, before they moved away.

Another relative we visited was Mother's brother Uncle Karl, who lived with his wife Alicia of Norwegian origin (Bergen), in San Francisco. She was thrifty. I remember that before us kids visited, she would wrap newspapers around the rungs of the chairs we would be sitting on to protect them from being scuffed. After the Nazis invaded Norway, she told us that she sent packages via the International Red Cross to relatives there.

Another was Mother's sister Louise, who lived with her husband Bill Vaughn and two children. In the 1930's she died of pneumonia, we were told, whereupon Bill, with the young children, moved to Southern California, and we lost contact.

My father's sister Louise sometimes visited us along with her husband Harold. Although Harold probably had some good qualities, what I remember most was his habit of criticizing us children, particularly me, for disagreeable eating habits. "You're just shoveling it in, aren't you?" Aunt Louise, though she could be critical also, won my heart because she was so attractive. She became a teacher, and then a principal, so she knew all the tricks kids could play, or excuses for not doing our chores. I referred to her in one of my recollections as "The Lie Detector."

One of my favorite Depression stories originated from Aunt Louise. She was looking out of the back door of her home in Riverside, California wondering how she would be able to accommodate her parents who were coming for dinner, as she was without the food from which a dinner could be prepared. Suddenly, she saw a hawk flying over the house with a duck in its claws had come to rest on the back fence. Seeing her chance, she rushed at the hawk, causing it to flap away, dropping its prey in its haste to escape. So she cooked a duck dinner.

Grandparents, we hardly knew. Dad's parents moved from Silver City, Utah to Riverside to be near their children, but I have little recollection of them. Mother's parents remained in Salt Lake, and we had little first-hand contact.

My sister Martha recalls our paternal aunt and uncle, the Pattesons, who lived near Riverside within an orange grove. She recalls how Uncle Pat once pulled down an avocado from a tree outside their house, giving it to her with some ketchup on it for her to eat. She found it to be a full meal. My recollection of the same citrus grove is of the smelly rotten egg that I once threw against the side of their tractor barn.

"Waste Not, Want Not" was an unspoken, but very much understood mantra, which underlay our lives. Unfinished portions were saved in the refrigerator to be used in soup the next day or the day after. I remember that once in the car we passed by a jumbled pile of used bricks on the roadside, my father braking to a stop. We loaded the car with as many of the bricks as the sagging springs would allow. Later, we would all be put to the task of scraping mortar from the bricks, while Mother and Dad laid them down to create a patio or walkway surface. They might wobble a bit when stepped on, but Mother assured us that they looked better than new bricks.

I don't remember any trips to the dentist; that would have been highly unlikely. My first acquaintance with a dental office that I recall did not occur until I was in the Army.

By about 1940, a new federal program that Mother had heard about enabled her to arrange for a mortgage so my parents could have a house built next door to our rented house on Pinehaven Road in Oakland, after paying $15 for each of two lots. She has described the details in her memoir "Recollections." We were finally able to have a telephone, and although it was a party line phone, it was definitely a step up. We still had a wringer washer and a septic tank with a field of terra cotta pipes needing frequent pine tree root-removal maintenance. But we had a water heater, and at about this time, garbage service.

Some people were particularly hard hit. Among them were the Dust Bowl refugees from the Midwest and south, some of whom settled in our neighborhood, probably without a steady income. I regret now our being very disrespectful and disparaging when we, like almost everyone, labeled them as Oakies and Arkies.

June 2022

BOB WILKINSON

Chicken Feathers

My recollections about our animal husbandry enterprise with chickens as we were growing up in Montclair are ones replete with sensory images. I recall the fragrance of chicken manure as I stepped through it. The unforgettable odor of wet feathers occasioned by dipping the freshly killed chickens in containers of hot water to facilitate de-feathering still clings to my nostrils. The fragrance of chicken feed—scratch and mash—was not unpleasant. I can still recall dipping into the large sacks and the sound of grain being poured into the feeders.

Gutting the chickens—no fun there in scooping out the entrails! Chores involved descending the hill, slippery in wet weather, to feed the chickens before school. It was an everyday necessity, of course. I also recall the cleaning and scraping of the chicken coop floor and the manure-encrusted hands resulting from it. Building the enclosed runway entailed using eucalyptus poles from our backyard, which were then joined with chicken wire. Chickens did not always live to produce eggs and meat. I remember many of them dying from disease or being killed by rats. I at least had the satisfaction of shooting one of the rats with my bow and arrow.

We witnessed the real meaning of the "pecking order" as Chicken A picked on Chicken B and so forth. The lowest ones on the pecking order were sometimes pecked bloody and looked scrawny from too little opportunity to feed unmolested.

Who can forget the bloody end for those chickens, which managed to live to become stew. Off with their heads! The executioner's axe did the job if the chicken held still long enough on the chopping block. The chicken episode came about, as I recall, partly because of the example of fresh eggs and fowl from the yard of Dr. Fornoff. It looked easy then as he handed us a few eggs from his well-kept henhouse and contented hens. The other impetus was undoubtedly the rationing of meat and eggs imposed by wartime scarcity.

I suppose it added up to our nutritional benefit, but I do not have any recollection of the pleasures of gathering eggs. I do not even have any pleasant memories of eating the chickens. Instead, I associate chicken meat of that era with stewed chicken, which I do not enjoy. With the memories of the gooey, mucky, smelly chores, it is a wonder that I like chicken recipes at all!

BOB WILKINSON

Tales Told, or Not Told, at the Dinner Table

Jonathan Gottschall's book about humankind, which he titled *The Storytelling Animal*, reminded me of tales from my mother. Most of the family stories told by her were on the theme of hard times, frequently illustrative of the stress and challenges of pioneer days in 19th century Utah. For example, her grandmother Eliza, one day grasping her three youngest children, including an infant, left her cabin and ventured into the fury of a severe snowstorm. The children barely survived, but she did not. Mother thought she might have ended her life because of despondency over its harshness and because her husband had taken on several more wives, as was the Mormon custom at the time.

However, one story was of much more recent vintage, dating from the 1920's, and told to me again when my mother heard that my wife and I planned to relocate to San Mateo. Mother had reminisced earlier about the days in her youth when she and friends in Salt Lake City considered it a special treat to enjoy a Saturday excursion by train to Saltair, a resort on the Great Salt Lake, where they could, after renting swim suits, float on the surface, buoyed by the heavy, salt-concentrated water. The main caution about the water in the lake was always to be careful not to dive into it or splash water in anyone's eyes, as it would sting intensely. That was their only experience with saltwater. It did not prepare her or my father for an adventure they took during their first married year in California, which happened to take place in San Mateo.

They thought it would be a capital idea one day to go camping at Coyote Point, rustic and undeveloped at that time, not a park as it is now, and only a mile's walk from where they lived. Lacking anything as sophisticated as a sleeping bag, they took a few blankets and found a somewhat level spot near the Bay to spend the night. They probably waded for fun in the unfamiliar bay water, and kept their breakfast food immersed in it to keep it cool. After bedding down for the night, they were lulled to sleep by the gentle waves against the nearby shore. Sometime during the night they were awakened by wet blankets as water was, to their amazement, spreading over them. This was not what they were familiar with at the Great Salt Lake, water inexplicably rising up during the night, and were totally unprepared for tides. To escape, they had to clamber up a cliff in the dark without so much as a candle to light their way, their breakfast swept away. In subsequent years, our parents took us camping only in places considered safe like Big Basin, miles away from the unpredictable seashore.

Most of the stories my mother passed on were about her mother or her nine older siblings, nothing about her father, my grandfather. It was only much later that 1 ran across a typed account of his youth in pioneer era southern Utah in the 1860's. As a child, I might have complained one day about having to clean out the chicken coop or wash windows, but I could probably have been silenced by some of the stories about my grandfather. At only thirteen or fourteen, he was told by his father to take a mule team and wagon with some barrels of water, along with flour and bacon into the desert to re-supply a couple of thirsty desert rats who were digging a well. His father had been told by a man with a water witch that a well could be successfully dug there, a spot which lay about halfway along a desert trail. It was a time-saving cut-off for people heading farther west, but a dangerous route because of no water. The bones of unsuccessful travelers were sometimes found on that trail. His father, as head of the pioneering mission, had persuaded two men to dig a well there.

His son prepared for the trip as he had been told, drawing water from the nearby river and loading it into the wagon. It was a difficult enough trip through the desert sun and sand, but part way on the twenty-five mile errand to the two men, he was intercepted by some Indians from a nearby tribe, armed with bows and arrows, who teased him and tipped the water from the barrels into the sand, taking his lunch, which forced him to return home, mission unaccomplished, only to be sent out once again by his father to complete his errand.

BOB WILKINSON

What my mother also didn't tell me, and what I only found out as I read further in my grandfather's account, was that after several such trips, he became so weary and despondent from these and similar chores, that he flatly refused to continue. He threatened that if forced to load up the mules and wagon again, he would take them, not to the men in the desert who could die as far as he was concerned, he said, but instead take off to California. His father was shocked at such unheard-of disobedience, but finally with his wife's advice, gave in. However, he was unable to recruit any men in their community to take his son's place, despite the offer of pay, forcing the well diggers, without any provisions, to abandon their ill-advised labor. By then, they had reached a depth of sixty feet without finding signs of any moisture.

My grandfather compiled these and other stories of youthful hardship and danger in 1918, when he was in his 60's, after years of immobility because of severe arthritis. My mother did not remember any time when he was not forced to use crutches or wheelchair to move about. I assume that he must have told some of his stories to his children about his more active and adventurous time of life, but I am unsure why my mother never told any of them to us. Perhaps, as the youngest of ten children, she missed out on the stories because he had grown tired of repeating them, already having told them so many times to the siblings who preceded her, or maybe the stories seemed too incongruous with her sense of him, in her experience, as always an invalid.

Our treasured family memories remind me of the quote attributed to Muriel Rukeyser, a 20th century American poet, that "the universe is made, not of atoms, but of stories."

October 2015

Wagons Ho!

I don't remember having toys to play with as a child. It was the Depression, and gifts were probably mostly socks and other practical items of clothing. But behind our rented house on Pinehaven Road in the Oakland hills, there was something that inspired everyday imaginative play. It was an old covered wagon, the canvas top long-gone, but the wooden box, iron fittings and some wheels still in place. The front could be manipulated from side to side as though the oxen were still hitched to it and turning the wagon.

It afforded opportunity for recreating pioneer days as described to us by our mother, whose grandparents came across the plains to Salt Lake. We fought off hostile Indians, and fended off thundering herds of buffalo and failed robbers, sometimes with the help of my cap gun obtained by sending in coupons from boxes of corn flakes.

Although we might have outgrown it eventually, some parts of the wagon lived on. One wheel graced the front of the cabin that our parents eventually acquired in the Russian River area. Also, years later, my father made a wooden tool box for me, resurrecting one of the old wagon metal parts as the handle. It survives to this day in our garage.

BOB WILKINSON

Schoolyard Games We Played

My elementary school in Oakland had no baseball field. In fact, not only was there no baseball, I don't think I ever saw a ball of any kind during recess while I was there. Instead, what I remember was what I could now designate as "pocket games," the supplies for which we kids brought to school.

Marbles

In elementary school everyone had a few marbles in an old sack, often a Bull Durham tobacco sack, which would be pulled out of one's pocket at recess. The first thing to be done for some of the games was to describe a diamond, or circle, in the dirt. This configuration was called "fish" because of the elliptical shape of the boundary marked with the end of a stick. Sometimes it could be in a circle, depending on the whim of the most assertive boy. The ground surface would be smoothed and pebbles removed.

One of the contestants, or sometimes more than one, would place several marbles within the circumference, and the first player assumed his shooting position by "knuckling down," holding his special "shooter" between the thumb and forefinger. The opponent(s) would take up a position outside the diamond with their favorite shooter.

The person who placed their marbles within the diamond would often try to half bury them in the dirt while positioning them in order to deter the shooter. This could provoke an argument. The shooter was a special marble treasured for its slightly larger size and weight and therefore its extra mass, useful in imparting a velocity to any marble it struck. Anyone whose knuckles were caught in the act of shooting while over, or touching, the line, came in for a good yelling. You could keep the marbles that were shot out of the circle or diamond (keepsies). There were some special rules about whether a shooter could be kept if left in or knocked out of the diamond.

Another marble game was lagging—that is, trying to toss your marbles closer than anyone else to a line drawn in the dirt. The order of play was also determined by lagging marbles toward a line drawn in the dirt; the person whose marble landed closest went first.

Marbles came in various colors and designs, and had a special nomenclature. A very special steel marble, a metal ball bearing, was called a steelie. It was sometimes considered outside of the limits of game use, but I remember using them as shooters. Some heirloom marbles from Dad's boyhood were made of agate (aggies). It seems I still have some of them. There were also "cat's eyes."

The size of one's marble pouch waxed or waned depending on success or failure at recess. My marbles were carried in Bill Durham tobacco sacks obtained from my pipe-smoking father. Consequently, one of my jeans pockets smelled of tobacco, while the pocket carrying the milk tops often had the fragrance of slightly sour milk, at least in between laundry days.

Milk Tops

We always played milk tops at recess. This popular pocket game required us to swipe the tops from milk bottles delivered to our back door every other day. I'm not sure what my mother did to replace the missing cardboard tops, but I accumulated as many of the tops as I could carry in my pocket to school. During recess we would gather beside the portable classroom to compete. The rules were that a top was dropped to the ground by the first boy. Then the next one would hold a top at eye level and attempt to drop it so that it would cover the first top. If one were successful, he would claim both tops, a gain of one trophy. There would be arguments, of course, about whether the top was covered or was just on the edge. This would continue until the bell signaled the end of recess. I found a few milk tops from this no-cost game in the basement (not of boyhood vintage), which brought back some of this memory.

BOB WILKINSON

An Englishman once claimed that leaders of the British empire learned their life skills on the playing fields of Eton. I wonder what kind of milk bottle tops they played with.

Balsa Glider

Balsa wood gliders were a nickel or a dime. At recess the object would be to try to hit someone else's glider in the air with your own. There were always some special ways to fix your glider so that it would fly with more loops, or with more force, and have more impact on other gliders. We were always trying to retrieve them from the roof of the school building. One measure of prowess with the glider was to be able to sail it farther than anyone else. This led to some home-constructed models or more expensive models with longer wing spans.

Boxing and Wrestling

Unofficial sports occasionally erupted during recess, like boxing and dirt wrestling when someone was insulted or otherwise provoked. I can remember scrambling in the dirt during one such wrestling match, fortunately ending at the first round by the sound of the school bell. The matches usually ended with the first round, because only rarely did the personal animosity continue 'til lunch time. Insults and teasing were common place, like "Jim has cooties," which was sometimes true, to the distress of the person afflicted with head lice.

All of these games were the province of boys. Girls did other things, I suppose, like hopscotch played on squares drawn with chalk, jump rope, or playing on the monkey bars, nothing of interest to us.

I assume that inside the portable school buildings equipped with blackboards and potbellied stoves something important must have taken place. Otherwise, how would we have learned that the capital city of California is a place called Sacramento, or about the principal product of Holland, or the year Columbus "discovered" America. But our real life took place outside, between the buildings or on the playground.

Baseball
In the glow of the World Series, I have tried to recall when I first became aware of major league baseball, or even of the game itself. Baseball at that time was a distant, adult kind of activity, knowledge of which was gleaned from overhearing fathers' and uncles' conversations or from the baseball cards that were on the back of nickel bubblegum packets purchased at the small candy store owned by the community barber. These were collected and traded like blue chip stocks on Wall Street, although there were few players whose names meant anything to us, other than Babe Ruth, probably. Actually learning how to play the game was a skill learned later in junior high where the school actually had a field with bases marked out on it and bats and balls to go with it.

I eventually heard that there was a baseball team playing across the Bay in San Francisco at something called Seal Field, and the name DiMaggio was a baseball player who people sometimes talked about. By that time my "pocket games" had long since faded away, along with my devotion to kid radio programs like the Lone Ranger, and the Wheaties "Breakfast of Champions" cereal coupons for ordering cowboy cap pistols. Little League did not arrive in my life until our firstborn became of sufficient age. While I may have missed out on baseball in my early childhood, as a parent I became a fan to the extent that I could be oblivious to what I was eating for dinner while the Giants battled for the title. Let's toast second chances!

October 2012

BOB WILKINSON

A Song of Men, Metal, and Wood

Hanging from a nail on my chaotic, cluttered garage wall amidst the dust of decades hangs, like the sword of Damocles, a five-foot long, two-man whip saw. Edged with sharp, two-inch long teeth and shiny with oil to repel the ravages of rust, this metal remnant of Paul Bunyan's era rests there to bring to life the seventy-year-old memories of backyard toil among the eucalyptus trees of my childhood. The sweat-stained wood handle on one end and the "W" burned into the larger handle at the other claim ownership of both tool and recollections.

On occasional Sundays, my father, whose six-day work week in an office, devoid of physical effort, looked forward to outdoor work to restore his soul. He would announce that we were going to cut down one of the excess trees on our property in the Oakland hills and convert it into logs to be maneuvered, with the help of block and tackle, into position to form a bulwark for a level spot on our sloping hillside.

So, with myself at one end of the saw and my father at the other on the far side of the tree, we would alternately pull this steel saw back and forth, to and fro, the metal teeth emitting music that resonated as an instrument, not unlike a bow scraping against a wooden cello, while a satisfying stream of saw dust shot out from the cut and accumulated in a pile on the dirt. It was important to pull, not push on one's handle to avoid buckling the flexible saw, so that my strenuous pull was followed by a brief respite as my father leaned back with his pull.

Eventually the back and forth rhythm of the singing blade would become slower and more strenuous as the saw bit further into the moist tree tissue, causing a binding friction that resisted our lagging efforts. Then, it would be removed and set aside while my father applied an axe vigorously to the tree or log to widen the cut. Meanwhile, I could rest amid the odor of damp eucalyptus saw dust and the clop, clop of the axe. Then the saw once more to the cut, back and forth, its own song of labor ringing throughout the canyon.

With fatigue and boredom, I once grew careless pulling the saw, with the painful result that my leg, having moved too close to those sharp metal incisors, felt the bite of the teeth. My blood and twelve-year-old tears mixed with the sawdust. The resulting scar on my thigh persisted for many years as a reminder of that day of lapsed attention.

Parenthetically, I am now inclined to wonder if my life-long indictment of eucalyptus trees—that alien fire hazard species, notorious thief of moisture in the garden, prolific litterer of leaves and bark—is perhaps more related to the backyard toil they exacted in my childhood with the two-man saw.

But that tool with its business-like teeth, unmindful of and uncaring of victim, whether tree or flesh, is a symbol of a lost, perhaps honorable, but unlamented form of labor. Thankfully, it is destined by virtue of present day power-driven chain saws to remain at rest forever as an antique. Perhaps someday the saw will provide the surface for an amateur painter who will describe on it an idealized forest scene and then hang it on the wall of some rural café which offers Paul Bunyan roast beef sandwiches and Blue Ox soup. It may be in the company of other equally quaint but discarded hand tools collected in an attempt to engender a nostalgic woodsy atmosphere for customers. But to the knowing user, it speaks less of an idealized past than of singing metal, sawdust, sweat, and scars.

BOB WILKINSON

Adolescence: "Fake It 'Til You Make It"

My adolescence was life as a fake, no matter what seriousness I put to it. It was make believe, play acting. Take for example the time in the late winter and spring of 1942 when I was deputized as an air raid warden at age fifteen. Wartime anxiety was at its peak at the time in the aftermath of the attack on Pearl Harbor, the fear being that Japanese planes would be bombing us on the West Coast next, that we were virtually defenseless, and that our safety depended on volunteer watchers who would scan the skies to detect and alert us to the presence of planes from enemy aircraft carriers.

At an Air Raid Warden meeting at our local school, one night we were handed arm bands, flashlights, white helmets, and unbelievably, a gas mask. My assigned post was a few hundred yards from our home in the Oakland hills, overlooking the Bay and San Francisco in the distance. We were told by some official in secret, in order to raise our anxiety and awareness, that we were to look out for not only Japanese planes but also Japanese balloon bombs, some of which had already fallen in the Northwest.

So, after dinner I would ostentatiously assemble my paraphernalia and head for the lookout post up the road, all household lights and street lights blacked out by that time, so it was very dark, adding to the drama. A neighbor's dog usually set up a fierce barking just as I passed; otherwise all was quiet. Exactly what I was to do if I spotted a plane, and how I would recognize it in the dark as an enemy plane, was unclear. Probably if I saw something suspicious, I was to run home and use the telephone—a multi-party line, at that—hardly a strategy for a modern day Paul Revere.

It was all pretense. Perhaps it helped our morale by lending us the feeling, however fake, that we had some control over our fate, and maybe, in its way, helped pull the community together in the common struggle. This make-believe lasted but a short time until the sea and air battle of Midway put some distance from fear of bombing. The Battle of Midway, which took place June 3–6, 1942, was a World War II naval battle fought almost entirely with aircraft, in which the United States destroyed Japan's first-line carrier strength and most of its best trained naval pilots.

When I was a seventeen-year-old senior in high school, I was hired as a reader by the biology teacher, my primary duties being to correct the homework of students in her junior biology class. I took the papers home after school and spent many hours going over the student work, pretending I knew what I was doing when actually I had to laboriously page through the textbook to find the answers. At least I learned, or re-learned the lessons that my teacher assumed I had mastered in her class the year before, a certain degree of pretense on her part, for sure.

One summer, hired to rid a vacant lot of weeds by burning them, I pretended to understand how to follow instructions given rather casually by the owner on how to set and control a fire that would eliminate the weeds, but not burn down the wood fence that surrounded it on three sides, or the stores and homes close by.

June 2015

BOB WILKINSON

My Encounter with the Sheriff of Nottingham

"What do you have in that pouch, young man?"

The question came from a policeman who had brought his patrol car to a stop next to me at the side of a rural road in the Oakland hills. He leaned out the window with the bare hint of a smile and pointed to the homemade, fringed leather satchel strapped to my belt. In my left hand I held my bow; several arrows protruded above my shoulder from my patchwork quiver, fashioned for me by my grandmother. On my head was a cap with a ruffed Scrub Jay feather protruding from the brim.

I had just stepped down onto the nearly deserted road from a tree-covered hillside where I had been wandering on that early Sunday morning, a good place and time to live out in solitude my-twelve-year old's fantasy of Robin Hood and his merry men. Thickly covered with pine and eucalyptus, this was my Sherwood Forest. Deerskin-clothed fellow archers lurked just out of sight behind trees and bushes with Little John and the Friar not far off. I am not sure about Maid Marian; at my age she may not have figured prominently in my imagination.

Stalking under the dark forest canopy, my arrows were aimed at just about anything, but principally tree trunks. However, when I saw a Brown Towhee resting on a twig close to the ground, I took a bead on it, never expecting to hit it. To my great surprise, the arrow struck its target, something that had never happened to me before. A little regretful at my killing of a harmless bird, I nevertheless picked up its lifeless and still warm feathered body. Although perhaps not a majestic stag to be roasted over a fire and shared at the evening meal with the other members of Robin Hood's gang, I could still consider it a hunting trophy anyway. This was what bulged from the pouch at my side and was the object of the policeman's untimely curiosity.

The prospect that the Sheriff of Nottingham would apprehend me for poaching in the King's game preserve could not have aroused more consternation. I was sure I was going to be arrested and my parents notified of my crime for shooting a bird. Desperately, I stammered out a lie.

"Oh, this? It's just an apple."

My face must have been a deep red, its expression every bit a guilty one, but the policeman said something else, long since lost to memory, and drove off, to my immense curiosity.

When I arrived home, I hurried to find the shovel in the garage, and found a place far to the rear of the backyard to bury the evidence. I would not mention the encounter with the police or the bird to anyone.

It was only many years later that I wondered if the policeman, bored with his uneventful Sunday morning patrol on a nearly deserted road, saw me in my patched jeans, bow and arrow equipped, as a possible diversion, and perhaps an encounter with a memory of his own boyhood. He didn't know that his opening question was to be interpreted, not as a friendly conversational gambit, but as an arrow striking directly into the heart of a guilty conscience. Where had been the courage of Robin Hood at my hour of greatest need?

June 2010

BOB WILKINSON

My Mother the Fight Promoter

There is one five-word sentence that I remember my mother speaking, more so than any other complete sentence that I can recall, although I must have heard many thousands of sentences from her in a lifetime. These words were decidedly violent in meaning. It was when I was ten or eleven years old and our family was in the backyard of our rented house in the Oakland hills.

But first, I must say that my mother was the gentlest of people. She could not bear to listen, as my father and I did, to any radio broadcast of a prize fight. When there was a heavyweight match between Joe Louis and someone else, perhaps Max Schmeling or "Two Ton" Tony Galento, she would insist that the door between the radio and the kitchen be closed, and she would insulate herself from the broadcast with the sounds of housecleaning or dishwashing. This was despite of, in the case of the Louis-Schmeling match, a great deal of international attention because of Hitler's Nazi prestige publicly being staked on Schmeling, a German heavyweight champion. Later on, she could not participate in the butchering of chickens that we raised during wartime. She couldn't tolerate any roughhousing by us kids. So, the astonishing words of aggression she used that day sank into my memory as though chiseled in polished granite.

I am not sure what we were doing in the backyard that day, perhaps weeding the garden and raking up the leaves from the eucalyptus that grew so abundantly nearby. A strange man saw us from the street and walked down the hill to where we were standing. It was very uncommon that anyone would find their way on foot up our road, half a mile uphill from the nearest bus stop and about ten miles from downtown Oakland. He would have had to pass the dwelling we called the Tarpaper House because of its partial completion, and which housed a large family, refugees from the dust bowl who we referred contemptuously to as Oakies. He would have passed the "Blindman's House," with its herd of mangy dogs, a canine enclave where my own pet preferred to hang out, much to my chagrin and jealousy. The street was called Pinehaven Road, although it was more eucalyptus than pine, and if it was a haven, it was for those seeking low rent.

Occasionally, a man with a horse-drawn wagon shouting "Old pots, pans, bottles, rags!" would find his way up the road; Pacific Heights or Nob Hill it was not. The stranger engaged my parents in conversation, but while doing so, stood behind me and put his arms around me, then inserted his hands down inside my trousers. It made me uncomfortable enough to move away from him.

After the stranger left, I told my parents what had happened, not thinking too much of it, just that I thought it was unusual. Upon hearing it, however, my mother exploded. She told—no, commanded—my father to go after him and "sock him in the jaw!" Those five words from my gentle-mannered mother shocked me, so much so that I would never forget the incident of molestation. I wondered whether she had, despite appearances, overheard some of the radio fight broadcasts to know what kind of blow to instruct my father to deliver to the stranger, on just what part of his anatomy to land his fist.

My father must have received his fight instructions from her with a bit of consternation. He was not a physically aggressive man, any more than my mother. Listening to a heavyweight fight did not mean that he was capable of imitating one. Yet his culturally appointed role as family protector required some action on his part. So, dutifully, he did get in the car, and a few minutes later returned to say that he had found the stranger and had told him to "Get out of the neighborhood, or else!"

As far as I was aware, there was no conversation between my parents about notifying the police, only intervention on a very personal and private level. Looking back, I don't know why my parents could not observe what the stranger was doing to me, as he made little attempt to hide what he was doing. Probably my parents were not looking at him, trying to ignore him in the hope that he would go away, which he ultimately did. Perhaps some measure of guilt for not being more observant and protective had something to do with the intensity of Mother's response.

Nothing was ever said about the incident afterward that I recall, but those five fighting words "Sock him in the jaw," delivered from a face twisted with emotion, have outlasted in my memory all other words spoken or written by my peaceful mother in the seventy years that I knew her.

January 2014

Grey Or Green, Color-Coded Cuisine

In my mother's cooking tradition—owing to a British legacy, probably—vegetables were to be cooked without mercy, and by that she understood it to mean until they turned limp and grey, that is, completely vanquished. Any vestige of greenness was indicative of neglectful undercooking. Consequently, I often gagged on green beans and broccoli that had yielded all traces of original color. She seemed to feel that original color was like ova, original sin. To eradicate it was the 11th commandment, supported by the fear of germs, that common enemy of all civilized mankind requiring lots of heat to neutralize, or at least in the tradition in which she grew up. My sisters and I tried different vegetable avoidance strategies, like hiding them in a napkin until we could sneak to the garbage pail when our mother wasn't looking. I don't eat broccoli cooked that way anymore.

The practice of well-cooked food was just fine. However, when it came to another of her English dishes, roast beef, my father's favorite meat dish, it was preceded in his tradition by a glass of scotch and soda. I associate roast beef with Sunday afternoons when there was that tantalizing fragrance coming from the oven, and the likelihood of the roast being served with my mother's famous homemade chili sauce. We could anticipate another episode of that radio drama, "One man's family." I don't eat beef anymore, regrettably, because of modern day dietary admonishments, but when I detect its odor in the air near a restaurant, it almost causes my feet to turn sharply in that direction as shreds of memory come rushing back.

At Christmastime, English tradition required my mother to prepare plum pudding, which was served in dramatic flambé style after the lights had been turned low. I don't eat that anymore either, not because of any dietary prohibitions, but because I have not the slightest idea of how to prepare it, and also perhaps because it seems too much like appropriating one of my mother's closest possessions.

BOB WILKINSON

Mother's bookshelves held volumes of Browning and other British poets; several pieces of Wedgewood china hung on the walls. One could say she felt part of the English diaspora, but she was at least two generations removed from that "Sceptered Isle." When someone mentioned to her once that she resembled a little the queen of England, she did not protest.

All of the tradition of English cuisine was to change for me when I became somewhat independent by marrying. I had the good luck of finding someone with an entirely different tradition for cooking veggies. My bride's style was to cook broccoli and green beans very slightly so that they retained their color and crispness. I recall how they awakened me to the realization that they could taste surprisingly good. No surreptitious trip to the garbage pail was ever contemplated. However, my mother must have felt like she had truly lost her son when she dined at our table early on in our marriage. What? Green peas that are still green? She might not have felt any more betrayed than if she had found a fly in her soup. Horrors! Or, as the queen might have said, "We are not amused!"

May 2015

A Squeeze In Time

On a hot mid-summer day in 1939 along the black asphalt highway traversing the table flat Nevada desert, heat waves formed ephemeral water-like mirages shimmering in the distance. At about noon, a bag lunch, packed in Salt Lake City at the home of relatives, was opened and dry sandwiches passed around, my father nibbling on his portion while holding the warm steering wheel. Water was distributed in paper cups and soon was consumed in the thirstiness of the day. Three oranges were eaten, two others put aside by my mother for a later time when they might be much needed and more appreciated, which seemed to be a true example of my mother's Victorian principle of delayed gratification.

Green, gray sagebrush stretched away on both sides of the road into the featureless distance. Jackrabbit road kill speckled the two-lane highway. On the far horizon a brown, bare mountain range hovered, never seeming to loom any higher or closer as the miles rolled by. The 1932 Buick carrying my parents and the three of us children rolled on through the mid-afternoon sun. Air conditioning consisted of open windows to catch whatever relief the moving air could offer as it also sucked skin moisture away.

Then, when the heat seemed at its most intense, our forward progress fitfully slowed as the engine began to sputter and misfire, then catch again, but finally shudder to a stop. My father pressed the starter several times, but the engine descended into a deathly, coma-like silence. Without forward movement, the air in the car quickly became stifling hot. Outside, the quiet of the desert was complete except for the approach of a distant truck, which soon roared past without slowing.

Dismounting from the car and raising the side of the hood, my father peered inside to examine the hot engine for clues to its revival. Water in the radiator hissed and bubbled under its cap. "Vapor lock," he soon announced as a probable cause. This meant waiting until the fuel line had cooled sufficiently to permit gasoline to flow to the engine without the liquid vaporizing first. With the heat of the engine inside the hood and the desert sun bearing down on the outside, the prospect of cooling the line seemed to portend a long-term desert wait. "If only we had brought more water," my father lamented, "we could have cooled off the fuel line by pouring liquid over it." I am sure ominous visions of desert desperation passed through my parents' minds, fueled by the oft-told stories from their pioneer forebears of Utah life in the mid 1800's crossing desiccated landscapes in ox carts.

After a few moments' hesitation, my mother remembered the two oranges stowed away for later relief for our dry throats. As much as those oranges might have been enjoyed for their moisture-giving quality to ease our thirsty mouths, she offered them to my father, who turned them over in his hands while judging in his mind the relative value of family thirst measured against the needs of the engine which, if not restarted soon would mean very dry mouths for us indeed. After a few moments hesitation, he cut open the precious oranges with a pocket knife and squeezed them, one at a time, precious drop by drop aimed carefully over the brass fuel line, the moisture running down the hot tube, hissing as it drained off against the greasy engine block, a kind of citrus therapy that might have warmed the heart of that Nobel Prize-winning scientist and vitamin C advocate Linus Pauling.

A few minutes later, the starter was tried again, the engine caught, and with a collective sigh of relief we were off, this time our thirst almost forgotten with the satisfaction of being under way. Oranges, for years after that day, carried for us the memory of a sacrificial squeeze in time and the inherited resourcefulness of descendants of desert pioneers.

SEPIA-TONED ARCHIVES

BOB WILKINSON

"Draft Dodger" No Longer

My Day At The Draft Board

"Greetings! Your draft status has been revised to IA effective immediately, and you will shortly be instructed by your local draft board to report for induction into the United States Armed Services."

So read the form letter that emerged after I, not quite nineteen years of age, had anxiously ripped it from its official-looking envelope deposited in our Berkeley mailbox. Why now? The first atomic bomb had just been dropped on Japan, and the war appeared to be finally nearing the end. At my initial draft board physical ten months earlier, my spectacle-framed eyes had been pronounced too defective to trust their owner with a gun. For the same reason, I had been turned down for a university medical training program under military auspices. But here was my draft notice. Was there some mistake?

I had seen several friends and acquaintances from high school go off to the Army or enlist in the Navy as their draft numbers had come up. Lew, a particularly close high school friend, was now completing infantry basic training. I was one of the few male students left in my University of California classes, and I felt conspicuously unpatriotic, my honor and manhood in question, to still be there among all the girls. I had completed mandatory Reserve Officers' Training Corps (ROTC) training with uniform, mock rifle drill, and close order marching; other class members were already on active duty. So, alongside the anxiety produced by the letter, there stirred also, at first, barely acknowledged excitement and relief. I was going into the Army! I'm not 4-F any longer! 4-F was the U.S. Selective Service classification used to designate a person physically, psychologically, or morally unfit for military duty. No more would I be a "draft dodger" in others' eyes. I could picture myself resplendent in uniform and no longer a mere spectator of the most important world event of my life.

At my age, the war had been perceived as a heroic enterprise. Of course, there were casualties reported in the news, but in the movies it was all so bloodless and victorious for us. I wanted to be part of it.

BOB WILKINSON

As I entered the family kitchen, letter extended but feelings withheld, I immediately discovered that this eager sense of anticipation was not shared by my mother. To her, a draft notice meant handing over her only son to some ruthless force which she couldn't trust or control. "Draft notice? How heartless! We will see about that!" was her thought.

The local draft board was soon to experience my mother's determination. In she strode, with me reluctantly in tow, as she proceeded to plead my case, marshalling her arguments forcefully and growing more emotional as her presentation and attempts at charm appeared to fall on unappreciative ears. I, as her foot-dragging client, hung back, and feeling deeply embarrassed by her unwanted advocacy, offered no arguments of my own. I was unable to soften my mother's campaign on my behalf. At that stage in my life, it would have taken more independence than I possessed to stand against my mother's determination.

My chagrin deepened and my face reddened when a grey-haired, stern-faced woman member of the draft board arose from her chair and upbraided me for being unwilling to do my part for my country when so many others had served and sacrificed. I could only flinch in humility and slink out the door as my mother's further protests were cut short by an official who closed off further pleading and growled that I would hear from them very soon.

When the expected letter arrived from the draft board, a small concession had been made: a brief postponement of the induction date. By this time, the war in the Pacific was over, so my mother felt her efforts to save her son from the heartless military had achieved something. But having already proudly announced my imminent departure to friends, I was not feeling grateful about the stay of induction; now it seemed a major benefit of military service would be a chance to get away from home. Such was the foundation for my patriotic service in uniform.

Army Justice

When I was drafted in 1945—not by the NFL, but by Uncle Sam—I expected to have to adjust to the regimen and culture of Army life, blissfully unaware of what that entailed. But a few months' exposure to barracks living and to staff sergeants took care of that. What I had not anticipated learning about was the culture of Southern life in these United States. This came about when the unit I was assigned to, Headquarters of the Ninth Air Force, then near El Paso and recently returned from overseas, was ordered across the country to an air base in South Carolina.

In the unfathomable wisdom of the Army, I had been assigned to the Judge Advocate's office. This was the branch of service which reviewed all court-martials for that Air Force, whether it was soldiers who had gone AWOL (absent without official leave) or who had gotten drunk and stolen a jeep, or who had assaulted someone after a crap game. It was a window on the seamy side of life and justice, Army style. It was not long before I found some examples of injustice which lay beyond the purview of court martials, but not far from the building where I performed my duties.

The first was the complete segregation of Army soldiers. Black soldiers were assigned to their own units, ate at a different mess hall, were not allowed in the PX (Post Exchange, the military store), or the movie theater. This was not unique to the Army, of course. One day, out of curiosity, I left the base to explore what lay outside the gates. I found an impoverished rural African American community known as Skiptown. People sat on the front steps of rough, unpainted wooden shacks, a privy in back, water supplied only by one neighborhood well. In town, drinking fountains were of course labeled either colored or white, but on this well there was no need for such a designation. In later years I came to realize that I could have found conditions that were not much different in California farm worker communities.

BOB WILKINSON

In contrast to Skiptown, one evening I encountered at the bowling alley four or five German-speaking men in civilian clothes learning how to bowl. It was now 1946, and I learned that these men had been Luftwaffe pilots or technicians, our sworn enemies of only a year earlier. I later learned that they had been swept up by the Army in Germany to prevent them from falling into Soviet hands so that they could coach some of our C46 pilots on how to, while still in flight, snatch gliders from the runway. They had the run of the base denied our African Americans; it would probably not have seemed inconsistent with the Nazi culture they left behind.

Against this backdrop, another incident of justice played out, which, although taking place in civilian life in the nearby town, reached deep into our Army life and affected many of us, both Southerners and Northerners.

In the nearby town of Greenville, a Black man had been lynched. This was not so unusual, I gathered, but what was unusual and historic was that a man had actually been arrested for the crime and was awaiting trial. It was not the lynching itself, but the trial which plunged the community nearby, as well as the barracks, into conflict.

Among us draftees, we were not always aware of the region of the country from which we hailed, except perhaps in the case of the guy from Texas who automatically acquired the nickname of Tex. Few others were labeled with their state of origin. Being from California, I was sometimes regarded with cautious curiosity by those who knew where I came from. With the news about the trial disseminating through the barracks like no other news had, it quickly became apparent who was a Southerner. There could have been all sorts of world crises or significant sports news without receiving any attention in the barracks, but this event was soon taken up loudly and aggressively.

No cuss words were left unspoken in the Southerners' fierce opposition to the trial; the intrusion into the community of "Yankee" reporters sent to cover the story came in for the most virulent attack.

Those of us from "Northern" states rose to the bait, with guys who had formerly been buddies yelling at one another across the Mason-Dixon Line. It was fortunate that no weapons were in the barracks or the reporters in town might have had a miniature Civil War to report on. There was even an echo of the controversy, although much more muted, among the officer lawyers in the office of the Judge Advocate General where I spent most of my day.

In due course, the jury in town returned a verdict of "not guilty." Southerners celebrated by jeering at the rest of us, who could only mutter to ourselves.

Eventually, the barracks returned to its normal state of enlightened conversation—fantasies about exploits with women last weekend, or on pay day where to have the crap game.

While I might be forgiven at that time of my life for looking at the experience with some feeling of holier than thou, at least twenty years were to elapse before, back home in California, it became illegal to discriminate. The Fair Housing Act of 1965 prohibited racial discrimination in housing with the purpose of preventing discrimination and reversing housing segregation, which had been generally supported by real estate agents. This law only passed because enough people went door to door gathering sufficient signatures on petitions to place the issue before the voters.

Ironically, it was the armed forces which desegregated first, in 1948 by Harry Truman's executive action, about a year after my discharge, so I was not in a position to experience it. It was accomplished without congressional or popular vote, and years before Selma. After my experience in the Army, it is hard to imagine that it could have gone smoothly, or that Truman didn't have to face opposition from the rank and file at the Pentagon before taking action.

The arrest, beating, and blinding of African American veteran Isaac Woodard by police in Batesburg, South Carolina in February 1946, hours after his honorable discharge and while still in uniform, caused a nationwide uproar. In 1948, heeding pressure from Black civil rights leaders, and perhaps recognizing the importance of the Black vote in securing his political future, Truman was moved to overcome his deeply embedded, white supremacist Southern roots. Repudiating 170 years of officially sanctioned racial discrimination, Executive Order 9981 marked the first time a U.S. Commander in Chief used an executive order to enact a civil rights policy. Some perceived it as an act of courage on Truman's part. The "Buck stops here" president later famously administered another kind of Army justice, cashiering General McArthur for his expansion of the Korean war. Yet Executive Order 9981 was one of Truman's most important achievements, as it became a major catalyst for the civil rights movement, and other anti-discrimination laws that followed suit.

January 2015

A New York Moment

A recent re-run of the film "The Waterfront" with Marlon Brando caused some dusty fragments to fall out of my memory attic. It involved my first visit to New York City at age twenty. That first view of the city was through the plexiglass window of the bombardier's seat on a B25 bomber flying between my Army Air Force base in South Carolina and a base just north of New York. This macro vision of the fabled Big Apple was the beginning of a three-day holiday pass that was to also include an unforgettable experience at a very micro level.

It was 1946. Pete, my barracks room buddy, suggested that we ask for a pass to visit his family in Brooklyn. It would be his first visit home since his induction into the Army a year and a half earlier, and it would be my chance to see the city which existed for me only in the news or in the movies. As an added inducement, it was Christmas, a time better spent away from the base and its mess hall cuisine.

So, after securing a pass from the sergeant and checking out the mandatory parachutes from supply, we hitched a ride on a plane headed from our base to the New York area. After the flight landed, we took a bus which deposited us in Brooklyn, where, to my surprise, I heard Brooklynese actually being spoken by passersby.

"You mean that people actually speak that way? It isn't just in the movies or on the radio?" I asked, thinking of Brooklyn comedy characters heard on the radio, perhaps a Jack Benny or Allen's Alley program. Pete was much amused at my naiveté.

We were welcomed home by his mother, who seemed thrilled to see her only son after his long absence. His father, who I was told was a tug boat owner, had not arrived home yet from his waterfront business. After a few minutes he did arrive home, his greeting to my friend a brief, perfunctory one.

Judging from his breath, the father had apparently been celebrating the holiday before coming home, and continued to do so with the help of a bottle he took from the cupboard. Pretty soon I became aware of loud words from the father directed at his son, and then his fist flew out, knocking Pete to the kitchen floor while his mother covered her face with her hands. It was the end of the visit home for him, as we took our jackets and fled out the door into the cold New York winter wind.

Pete, nursing a bruised cheek and ego, seemed disinclined to talk about the conflict with his father or his family. I speculated on whether the fisticuff behavior by Pete's father was typical of how waterfront style authority was wielded in New York. We returned to the base by train, somewhat earlier than expected. It was to be many years before I would return to New York and my visit be unclouded by that first experience with my friend and his "on the waterfront" father. My first New York experience resulted in a real-life drama which had merged in my mind with images previously formed only by radio and film.

January 2014

SEPIA-TONED ARCHIVES

BOB WILKINSON

Crossing the Stream of Many Landscapes

Garlic, Red Wine, And Ginger

I am in the cluttered kitchen of a small men's co-op in Berkeley, several blocks west of the campus, outside the usual perimeter of the more recognized, better organized, student housing, in the low rent neighborhood, in 1949. The light slants in at an angle, indicating the lateness of the hour. It being Tuesday, I am the designated chef for the evening, but I am woefully unprepared for it.

Pulling on the rickety handle of the refrigerator door, I search its scanty contents in hopes of finding some source of culinary inspiration. The group of 8 - 10 fellow students living there will be expecting some sort of substantial meal within a few minutes to assuage their end-of-day appetites. One or two must leave soon for evening jobs; others must leave for the library. In fact, one or two heads have already peered around the doorway to assess the progress of preparations, since no cooking odors have found their way into their rooms.

The refrigerator collection of half-consumed jars and bottles on the shelves furnish no clues of any dinner that I can imagine. Then an idea from the past suggests itself: stew. As I tried to recall the ingredients that I had seen my mother use, but which I had never prepared myself, only consumed at the family dinner table, our landlord, who lived in the quarters above us, entered the kitchen to introduce a young woman friend. He cheerfully announced that she would be a guest for dinner, a gesture of dubious hospitality to the guest, indeed a triumph of faith over experience, it seemed to me.

Miss C., our guest, generously inquired if there were anything she could do to help out in the kitchen. Well! What an offer! "How do you make stew?" I asked.

Now, if she had any self-preservation instincts after that acknowledgment of naive unpreparedness, she would have certainly remembered that she had an urgent dinner appointment elsewhere. But she calmly and matter-of-factly proceeded to list some stew items: soy sauce, ginger, garlic, cooking oil, red wine, stew meat of course, and two or three vegetables. We had none of these items in stock other than a sad-looking potato or two, but she reminded me that a corner grocers was just down the street.

So, off l scurried, with the anxious, famished looks of the residents following me. When I returned, I saw that Miss C. had found and cleaned an appropriate pot. She promptly proceeded to place in it the garlic and oil, followed by the cubed meat and crushed ginger, and then the vegetables, which she also washed and sliced, as well as some wine.

By this time, encouraging cooking aromas were filtering through the rooms, and people were beginning to move eagerly toward their source. A tasty stew meal was soon served and enjoyed by a very much relieved and appreciative group. Miss C. was the heroine of the occasion, toasted with the wine left over from the stew. "Next Tuesday can you come for dinner again?" inquired one appreciative resident. I enthusiastically seconded the suggestion, seeing her as my Tuesday salvation.

Next Tuesday arrived and Miss C., my culinary mentor, did as well. This time I was realistically prepared with some ingredients for the meal. Better meals soon became a tradition on Tuesdays, and my cooking apprenticeship benefitted enormously.

Well, one thing followed another, and eventually it seemed wise to ensure that my culinary mentor should always be close at hand lest I suffer from malnutrition. So Miss C. and I were married, a courtship based not so much on the dance floor and flowers, but on garlic, red wine, and ginger.

The Test

I am not sure what I expected to encounter in my first introduction to a Hawaiian luau. Blossom, my bride, did not imply that this was a pass/fail examination for prospective future family membership, but the unspoken message was that, since it would be my first introduction to many family members and close friends, I could influence my acceptance by participating.

Sounds of a slack-key guitar floated through the lanai as we entered the flower-decked hall amid greetings, some in pidgin, and joined the throng of people sporting shorts, sandals, aloha shirts, and *lei* seated at the tables. Just then, a pair of hefty Hawaiian men came through the entry bearing a roast pig on a tray. It was revealed later that when the pig had been carried up the outside stairs, it had become a victim of gravity and slid off the tray, bumping down the dusty steps to land ignominiously at the bottom. Happily, there was no disruption in enthusiasm for the pig or the feast as a whole.

Local beer was being consumed by some; others sipped more potent Okolehao or Mai Tais. "*Okole Maluna!*" or "Bottoms Up!" was the unfamiliar toast. Meanwhile, the business of dining began. First, *pu pus* were served, a peculiar word for a food it seemed, consisting first of a small quantity of a barnacle-like tidbit called *opihi*, laboriously scraped by Blossom's brother, I was told, from the lava rocks at the seashore, yielding a salty sensation to the taste buds. This was followed by *lomi lomi* salmon—fresh, uncooked, hand massaged and prepared with Hawaiian salt, tomato, and ice. Not at all like bass or catfish, I thought, but something one might get used to. I bravely dipped into the *limu*, or seaweed, which came next, followed by something of uncertain origins.

"You should like this. It's considered a special treat," Blossom said, not very reassuringly.

It is not diplomatic for a *malihini*, or mainlander like myself, to inquire first before tasting. Later, after savoring the unfamiliar dish, my ignorance was filled in by the revelation, shocking to me, that I had been eating raw squid, caught by my bride's scuba-diving cousin that morning, pounded with a rock and briny seawater, specially in my honor. I was grateful that my ignorance had preceded my eating of it.

For a person with my background on the mainland, a good meal consisted of roast beef, mashed potatoes, corn, jello, and apple pie. A really daring, pushing-the-envelope kind of hostess might include a slice of French cheese.

Poi came next in coconut bowls, a grey, pasty, muddy-looking and bland-tasting staple of early Hawaiian cuisine which the purists ate unseasoned, usually with two fingers. Less traditional diners like myself added soy or garlic sauce to obtain a little flavor, but didn't ask for seconds.

Before I could take a second breath, whole yams appeared, baked with the *piece de resistance,* the *kalua* pig, which had been placed that morning in a hot, smoking pit lined with pre-heated stones. Some were placed in the pig's cavity and covered with elephant ear leaves and leaves of the ti plant—the original aluminum foil—then burlap and earth. With appreciative smiles and shouts of *"Ono!"* the diners dove into the succulent pig. By this time, I was able to appreciate the true value of an Aloha shirt, which allows for the generous expansion of the stomach under critical circumstances.

But we weren't finished yet! Blossom's aunt had prepared chicken long rice, actually vermicelli, which I felt compelled to at least taste, after being told that it would be risking a mortal insult to not have a large portion. A sensation of something I was to become much more familiar with, ginger, invaded and set up quarters in my taste buds. I tried to look appreciative in the direction of her aunt, a woman with an ample figure, clothed in a large flowery *muumuu.* Silently comparing her to my svelte bride seated beside me, I wondered, however, if her girth represented the future for both of us.

Along with the cooked and prepared dishes, platters of pineapple and papaya appeared as a relief from the more unfamiliar foods. Dessert consisted of *haupia,* a pudding made from shredded coconut, coconut milk, and cornstarch prepared by an in-law and not to be refused, despite my very full feeling. I had to admit it was sweet and soothing to the mouth after so many new and different flavors. Not to be outdone, another relative had just brought in hot malasadas, a sugary pastry originating in the Azores and Madeira Islands, eagerly adopted by Hawaiians from Portuguese laborers who came to Hawaii to work in the sugar plantations.

My face must have betrayed the extreme condition of inner distress as the dishes piled up. I applied my napkin to my fatigued lips and, signaling my belief that this was the end of the feast, I pushed back my chair, anticipating the effort to arise, fattened but not defeated from the arena of my gladiatorial dining contest. My bride's teasing nickname for me had been "shark bait" in view of my pale mainland skin and newness to island ways. She nodded and squeezed my hand in approval of my gourmand efforts "so far."

"So far?" I inquired weakly.

"Wait 'til you taste *kulolo,* the taro pudding!" she exclaimed, as her cousin proudly plunked down a large portion on my plate.

Whoever said that the way to a man's heart was through his stomach perhaps had in mind not romantic advice, but something more dire—a warning about heart attacks.

BOB WILKINSON

Where Was I? (When Our First Child Was Born)

That was a question simmering in the mind of my wife Blossom, who was patiently waiting in the maternity ward at Provident Hospital, Oakland. As other fathers came and left, greeting their weary wives and exclaiming over their just-born, red-faced babies, she hopefully assured the nurse checking our child's vital signs, "Oh, he will be here soon." Meanwhile the clock ticked on as the visiting hour was slipping away.

Our first offspring, arriving in 1952, was prepared for as was no other of our subsequent three children. Red Cross classes were faithfully attended; bathing was practiced on doll babies; the "football hold" was mastered (although a soapy, slippery and squirmy baby turned out to be quite different); burping methods were rehearsed; and diapering was practiced with safety pins, the crib and baby blankets donated by friends and family. In my graduate social work classes I paid eager attention to child and personality development theory. We were going to be well prepared parents, no matter what anxieties lurking just beneath the surface might say otherwise.

After a mad dash to the hospital, the birth went well. I didn't suffer any pains at all, and it was a boy! Cigars were proudly distributed, and congratulations were offered. The next day I cut short my field work assignment in San Francisco to pay a visit to my new family in the hospital. I probably wasn't doing anybody any good there anyway. I took the train across the Bay Bridge, sent off with the well wishes of a clutch of fellow students.

Arriving at the appropriate stop, I dismounted the train, and crossed one street. Then at another crossing, I raced an oncoming car to the other side, just reaching the sidewalk before the car whizzed past, a risk-taking not out of the ordinary for me. Then a new thought revealed itself; I am now a father! I can't take chances with my life anymore! So, from that moment on, my young innocence and naiveté began to be replaced by something my earlier earnest preparations for parenthood hadn't accomplished—some awareness of the effect that my careless actions could have on my child, and my family.

Arriving at the hospital lobby, I, with my newly emerging consciousness, and a few straggly flowers plucked from someone's garden en route, mustered up whatever false confidence 1 could as a person who is to feel comfortable in a parent's skin, and eagerly inquired at a desk as to what room I would find my wife. The clerk looked through her card file for a while and asked me to please spell her name, as she couldn't find anyone by that name listed. I suggested that she must be in the maternity ward registry. The visiting hour was in progress and 1 didn't want to be late. The clerk looked again, with the same result.

The mental associations that then swirled through my brain included de Maupaussant's famous short mystery story about the man who, when he returned to his Parisian hotel to rejoin his wife, was told that no one by that name was there, nor had anyone ever registered by that name. With a significant glance, the hospital clerk then asked me what hospital she was admitted to. 1 thought that was a wholly unnecessary question.

"Providence Hospital, this one," I said, growing somewhat upset with the delay.

"Well," she confided with a smile, "you have come to Permanente Hospital."

BOB WILKINSON

The Brig On SS Fort Smudg

In the early sixties, in the backyard of our home on Holland Street in San Mateo, I constructed a playhouse in the form of a boat made from packing crates and other scrap wood scavenged with dubious legality from such places as the parking lot of a plant in San Carlos. It had a prow, a cabin, and hinged hatches which could be closed, and portholes on the side. It was enjoyed by everyone, including the neighbors. Taking a leaf from "Pogo," the comic strip, it was christened Fort Smudg after one of the many names given the boat propelled by Pogo and his friends in the Okefenokee Swamp. Pogo was one of our favorite characters; in fact he had been featured in Steve's birth announcement. Blossom sewed a flannel flag bearing the name but spelled without the "e" at Steve's insistence, because it was a silent e, he said. The flag was proudly run up the mainmast, or maybe the bowsprit. Only the children really know what fantasies were played out in this landlocked boat.

One day, when we were both returning from work and our babysitter Mrs. Gerken was still in charge, there was a faint cry for "Mrs. Guken!" coming several times from the backyard. My daughter Su-Lin came into the house to report that my other daughter Sunya was down the hatch. After tracking down the source, it was discovered that the cry did in fact come from Sunya, and she was trapped inside the boat, with a pleading look on her face, visible through a porthole. She had somehow irritated her brother Steve who was also playing in the boat, whereupon he had then imprisoned her by putting her down the hatch and nailing it shut with a hammer and nails fetched from the garage. So, for offenses allegedly committed on board ship, she had been effectively confined by the captain to the ship's "brig."

The "captain" was prevailed upon to release the prisoner by prying up the nails with the claw hammer.

Many years later, I repeated the memory of a playhouse in the shape of a boat in grandsons Weston and Glen's San Jose backyard, at Su-Lin's request. That boat was equipped with an escape hatch.

Backpacking: Escape From Sanity?

Hiking through wilderness, a non-competitive sport unless intentionally made so, has been my most satisfying physical activity over the decades. Yet it makes no logical sense. Why is it so compelling that the normal conveniences of home and safety developed over a thousand years of civilization's conquest of nature—a comfy mattress, heat-on-demand cooking stove, secure roof over one's head, food from a refrigerator, etc., are willingly—no, eagerly—left behind in favor of a heavy pack, a steep upward trail on exposed granite with oxygen-deprived lungs, wet clothing, balky cooking fire, eye-irritating campfire smoke, no electric light to read by, poor quality shelter, meals of basic grub, the possibility of sprains, burns, or injuries from falling, of hypothermia, of drowning in lakes, of bears stealing one's food when three days out, the relentless assault of mosquitoes, exposure to lightning storms, no plumbing, the sobering responsibility for the safety and well-being of children or others far from outside help? Of party members getting lost or separated in mountainous terrain? The realization that the mountains are unmoved by and oblivious to human despair or appeal? It defies any reasonable concept of sanity or comfort! In the words of someone quoted by backpacking writer Colin Fletcher, "Your legs must be stronger than your head."

The memory shelf of my backpacking is book-ended by two trips, one in my salad days when with two companions I reached Mt. Whitney from the west in 1948, and more than forty years later, a trip up into the Wallowa Mountains in North Eastern Oregon. Two trips could hardly be more different from one another than these.

MOUNT WHITNEY

The first trip was a youthful, naively planned excursion by the inexperienced, saved from serious privation only by the insistence of more adequate provisions by the mother of the other two hikers, and by the fortuitous meeting with some forest rangers halfway into the trip. And probably also by our youthful stamina and vigor.

BOB WILKINSON

In the days before foil-packed, freeze dried foods for the backpacker, there was something called multipurpose food, or MPF. It resembled the feed we used to give our chickens, and the odor wasn't much better. Dave and Tom Madden, my friends from Montclair days, were then living in Southern California, where I had gone for a visit. Their mother had prevailed upon us to take more of the MPF than we had planned, fortunately. The other food augmentation occurred at Crabtree Meadows, 10,000 feet elevation at the foot of Mt. Whitney, when some park rangers on horseback stopped in to use a small park hut nearby, meanwhile catching some trout from the stream flowing past our campsite. Early the next morning, the rangers were called on their radio and directed to depart immediately for a fire somewhere, and since they didn't have time to cook their trout, they very kindly gave them to us. Trout never tasted better after several days on MPF, and it gave us the additional calories needed to climb to the 14,000+ foot summit that day.

One other memory about the trip is still vivid, and it also is associated with food, an indication of what must have been on my mind during the trip: After laboring up and over Forester Pass (12 or 13,000 feet) we came upon a son and his father who proudly showed us why his pack was so big. He was carrying a large aluminum pot in which were arranged in an insulating bed of sawdust—like precious specimens—a dozen fresh eggs. I was not only amazed, but felt contemptuous about such gluttony and needless use of energy, when we were so virtuous and hardy as to subsist on our Spartan MPF. I am sure I was secretly jealous of their breakfasts.

On that trip, the jump-off point was Cedar Grove in King's Canyon. We climbed over three passes 12,000 feet high, traveling 114 miles in seven days, having to rush back to Berkeley so that I could register for classes the following day.

The view from Mt. Whitney was of seemingly unbroken peaks as far as one could see, an oxygen-deprived accomplishment. Although we had seen few people on our trip, during the last part of the climb, we found ourselves cast among several Los Angeles hikers who had come up the east side of the mountain on a day climb, at least one of whom came without water.

I recall a small wooden hut at the peak; inside was a large slab of ice, which must have accumulated when the door had been left open in winter. This trip was in early September.

WALLOWA MOUNTAINS

The later trip, up Hurricane Canyon along Avalanche Creek in the Wallowa Mountains of North Eastern Oregon in 1991, was an Elderhostel trip. We were supported by several llamas carrying our gear, and the llama owner who also cooked for us. Our day packs were light; we could enjoy the scenery without taking off heavy packs. We could watch bird life on the way, and upon arrival in camp were served gourmet meals, preceded by wine and cheese. That taste of luxury pretty much spelled the end to the strenuous kind of backpacking to which I thought I had been accustomed.

SOCK PUDDING

In between these two different trips were many with the children or with friends. One that Steve and Willy participated in is often recalled as the "sock pudding" trip. The second day out from Fallen Leaf Lake, after wakening to a nighttime accumulation of a few inches of snow, had been rainy, our boots sloshing through water-filled trails. That night at the campfire we attempted to dry out our soaked, freshly washed clothing. While the dinner stew cooked, Willy's socks were hung over the fire, until at one point they fell into the chocolate pudding simmering underneath. We didn't allow that mishap to affect our enjoyment of this much anticipated desert, but it did complicate the sock drying time.

Willy's socks figured into another trip, much earlier, with Bruce Bishop and Jerry Brock and some of their children, on a trip into Desolation Valley, west of Tahoe. When zapping dragon flies with his socks, Willy let go of one, which drifted out into the lake beyond reach of a stick, whereupon those with fishing poles cast their lures out to try to snag it. He recalls that Bruce managed to do so successfully, hauling it back as the catch of the day. Willy rewarded Bruce with a stick of gum.

THE GERALD FORD TRIP

The "Gerald Ford" trip, taken with Steve, Su-Lin, and Willy, was a five-day excursion into the Merced Peak area of the Sierra, beginning at a trailhead at the end of a dirt road fifty-six miles from the nearest trace of civilization. It was August 1974, and Willy was only eleven. The trip posed a challenge for someone his age. On the first night we pitched camp, we just threw down our sleeping bags on the trail, because the darkness overcame us before reaching our lake destination. I recall that some rodents nibbled their way into my pack and got into the food because we hadn't stopped soon enough to hang it out of reach while there was still light.

We explored several lakes: Vandenburgh, Lillian, Flat, Rainbow, and Anne. We scrambled cross country a few times, reaching an elevation of over 10,000 feet. We encountered few others on the trail. The trip was pretty free of problems, and we emerged at the trailhead tired, thirsty, and grimy, but pleased with the experience.

Driving out on the dirt road, it seemed to us like we were flying along, after moving only by shanks' mare for several days. When we eventually reached a small general store, we stopped to obtain some thirst-quenching beverages and ice cream. There, on a newspaper rack, a bold headline grabbed me: "Ford takes Oath." There were references to "President Ford." When we left civilization behind, Richard Nixon still lived in the White House. How pleasantly isolated we were from political distractions during those few days!

Colin Fletcher, author of *The Complete Walker* and *The Thousand Mile Summer,* mentions that happiness "has something to do with simplicity." The context refers to the pleasures of hiking and one's ability to absorb the sights, smells, and sounds of the trees and rivers without the distractions of everyday life. He also stresses the importance of taking only what you absolutely need, though a casual count of items on a checklist would run to at least sixty before taking food into consideration. Doing the checklist, accurately planning for food, studying maps, and estimating hours and days required to reach projected camp sites preoccupied me to the point of anxiety and sleeplessness. Once out on the trail, after the first night spent under the stars, such concerns fell away. I am sure John Muir would have had little patience with the checklists of modem day trips; he seemed to subsist on the barest of essentials, like bread crusts and tea.

Thoreau said that the swiftest traveler goes afoot; perhaps he meant, metaphorically, that we move less encumbered by the trappings and distractions of civilization when on our feet. The sound of the wind in a red fir forest and the vividness of the stars, minus the pollution of artificial lights, are among the pleasures to be savored in the mountains. One artificial light I well remember, however, was from a trip when the first satellite could be glimpsed overhead as a flashing, tumbling, moving point of light among the stars.

THE WIND RIVER MOUNTAINS

The Wind River Mountains of Wyoming provided the setting for a major trip that was partly recreational and part research-oriented. In 1987, at the age of sixty, I signed up for a program sponsored by the Audubon Camp of the West and the University of Wyoming. The purpose was to gather specimens and take observations of wildlife. I struggled with a pack weighing fifty-five pounds at the beginning of the eight days. This was recreation?

Periodically, the two other campers and myself, plus the three staff members, would lay down our heavy packs and break out the butterfly nets. With the packs released, we naturally felt almost lighter than air for a while. We must have presented a sight, pirouetting among the wildflowers and trees to pursue some elusive species. At night a net was deployed with a lantern to attract moths; we usually attracted mosquitoes instead.

The University of Wyoming found, from the specimens collected, that butterflies in these mountains existed in certain bands of elevation. So the elevation levels were dutifully recorded, along with notes about weather and clouds. Species of ants, beetles, and aquatic insects also went into our collecting jars.

Coming into view of a certain ridge, a staff member pointed to it in awesome, respectful tones, informing us that that was the spot where a wolf had been seen only two weeks earlier, a first sighting for that area in many years.

Earlier we had been shown a rustic log cabin hidden among the trees well back from a lake, where, judging from the beaver skin stretching boards and other paraphernalia, illegal trapping had been conducted in winter.

One day we stopped for lunch beside a beautiful stream. I noticed that opposite where we were sprawled, was a nest of water ouzels perched on a large, steep-sided boulder, a few feet above the water. This is the bird that so charmed John Muir, who felt that it cheered him more than any other. He observed it singing away in all kinds of weather, summer or winter, and dipping into the coldest streams.

THE DEAN FAMILY TRIPS

The first "Dean" family trip is memorable for the time we were trapped in a high open meadow when a lightning storm broke over our heads. The thunder crashed, the lightning struck, and we cowered as low as possible among some boulders, not wanting to offer any projecting heads to attract the electric currents. It was pretty terrifying in its intensity. That meadow may have been as beautiful as John Muir described them, but when prone face down among the grasses, trying to keep a low profile while the peals of thunder clang overhead, it's hard to properly admire the flowers only an inch away from one's nose.

The second Dean trip was taken with all five members of the Dean family, and with Willy, Su-Lin, and Steve. It was a six-day, five-night trip between the trailhead not far from the Deans' Strawberry Lake cabin and Kennedy Meadows, where one car had been left. Camping at scenic Emigrant Lake had a pretty-far-back-in-the-wilderness feel to it, as did climbing over Brown Bear Pass on the divide between Emigrant Lake and the canyon leading to our final destination. The views were rewarding, particularly as they helped us appreciate how remote we were, by our own efforts. Other hikers, even at this peak time, were very few at this remove.

I recall Jimmy Dean, the youngest and always the adventurous one, toying with a snake on the trail when I caught up with him, heedless of the rattles at the tail.

MARTHA, TIM and MYSELF

Martha wanted to do something to celebrate her son Tim's graduation (from high school, I think), so she, Tim, and I took a trip into Emigrant Basin. This time we had the support of a pack mule assist from a pack station near Strawberry Lake, so we carried only our day knapsacks the first and hardest day. That enabled us to hike farther the first day, and consequently, we penetrated farther into the wilderness area, exploring different lakes.

The accidental discovery of wildlife has helped to make pack trips worthwhile. Some of the memories that stand out more than the normal privations experienced, or the results of fishing: almost treading on the nest of a Chukar-like bird close to the trail, flushing a blue grouse in Wyoming, and watching the diving of nighthawks in Desolation Valley.

BOB WILKINSON

Calling Alfred Hitchcock

Scientists in California have been trying to understand why the frog population in the Sierra Nevada has dropped along with many important species of amphibians on the edge of extinction. If only they had consulted me years ago, I could have saved them a lot of trouble.

On our annual beginning-of-summer camping trip with my children about forty years ago, we pitched camp in the mountains next to a tributary of the North Fork of the American River. It turned out that the river held very little interest for the children in comparison to a brook nearby, narrow enough that it could be leaped over in one jump. More importantly, it vibrated with the *ribbet, ribbet* of croaking frogs. The hunt was on; there was a rush to collect frogs as though there had been a bounty placed on their slimy heads.

Large coffee cans used for campfire cooking were converted to portable frog ponds; anything which could conceivably contain a frog was pressed into service. It is doubtful that after the weekend, any frogs remained at large in the area. The fishing rods I had brought were ignored; after all, trout don't croak or jump from rock to rock.

When time came to return home, the naive, pushover driver allowed the campers to take their catch with them, provided they kept their promise to keep them securely sealed in their containers during the trip, a promise just waiting to be broken!

Before very long on the trip back, there were frogs under the driver's seat, and some perched on the back seat. I was afraid some would collect under the brake. At the first filling station, I stopped the car to take charge of the chaos. No sooner did I open the rear door, than a frog leaped out, closely pursued by my oldest son. It was probably only in search of a cool, moist place—the men's room—one hop ahead of me.

In retrospect, I am sure I had discovered a good story for Alfred Hitchcock if only I had seized on it.

"Picture, if you will, Mr. Hitchcock, the young biology graduate student hunched over the steering wheel of his station wagon, bearing several containers of frogs from his weekend collecting trip, headed down the mountain to deliver them to the research lab where he is working as an assistant to a world-renowned scientist. A thunderstorm envelops him in poor visibility, with a cliff on one side of the narrow road, and hairpin curves just ahead. Then, a deep, bone-rattling pothole shakes the car, and the frog container lids fly open. A sudden bolt of lightning illuminates the escape of the frogs into the front of the car, obscuring the windshield and overwhelming the driver to return the frogs to their canyon home.

"It would be a worthy sequel to your film *The Birds*, and a contender for the Oscars."

Sadly, hindsight is 20/20. Now, with Hitchcock unavailable, I will have to settle for writing an article for the *Scientific American* with my hypothesis and confession about the cause of the depopulation of frogs from the Sierra Nevada. With a nod to marine biologist Rachel Carson, I could entitle it "Silent Summer," although she would probably have condemned what transpired that weekend. It may cause a sensation, with embarrassment for the scientific community, which has been pursuing much more arcane explanations. Of course, I will have to use a pseudonym lest I entangle myself in the laws forbidding the taking of threatened or endangered species. The scientists can now turn their attention to the question which is more basic to the survival of amphibians: why do children like to collect frogs?

December 2012

BOB WILKINSON

Communication, the Key to a Happy Family

Open communication. That is the mantra of advice to parents from people who write such columns in the newspapers. Well, if I could have gotten my teenage daughter away from communicating with friends on the family telephone long enough, I might have been able to try communicating with her. While nowadays it seems that every child above the age of nursery school is equipped with their own cell phone, during the ancient times of which I speak, twenty years BC, that is, Before Cell, there were no such devices, unless perhaps they might have been used by the CIA or Dick Tracy.

The phone, that is, *the* household telephone, had to be shared by one and all in the family of six. There is nothing like the feeling of a close family atmosphere after school and in the evening, as everyone's attention is riveted on who is next to use the phone for absolutely urgent communication with friends. Who said that the kitchen is the center of the household? Yes it is if that is where the phone is located.

Time limits were tried, even using the kitchen oven timer.

Father might have tried to claim that there needed to be some free time for emergency work-related calls, but was interrupted as the phone rang again for one of the children. "It's about important homework," declared the recipient of the call, as this side of the conversation proceeded to sound a lot like a discussion of what was on TV at the moment. We noticed that some friends had a separate phone listing for their children. It seemed increasingly clear that there had to be a second phone line for use by the children, if the parents were to have any chance of equal access to the phone in the evening. It might have been worth the extra cost, certainly a better choice than going six blocks away to the nearest pay phone when ours was busy.

During the following days, arrangements were worked out with Pacific Telephone and Telegraph (remember them?) for a second line to be installed at a fee that we believed worth the benefit of phone freedom. A frank, good old Parent-Child communication ensued at the dinner table, in between phone calls, about the plan to have a new separate phone for the children, which had to be shared between them, leaving one phone free for us parents. "There will even be a separate listing in the next issue of the phone book," I stated. Any questions? All seemed to be understood. Bravo for good communication!

A few days later, someone came from the phone company, so that the additional line and phone was installed with extension cords for both phones. Problem solved! Phone freedom forever! That evening parental and child phone usage coexisted happily.

However, in the days that followed, the parents' phone continued to ring for one of the children. In the "family communication" sessions, it became apparent that, although their friends knew the children had their own line, they had gathered that it was preferred that they call on the parents' line to leave the children's line open for outgoing calls. More pointed discussions ensued, with communication open to a certain degree, that is, open in one direction mostly, from the top down.

With that problem dealt with, a somewhat improved, good order was restored. But several days later, during after school hours, Father tried to telephone home from work, but found that no matter how many times he called, there was only a busy signal, not only for the parental phone, but for both numbers.

Needless to say, later in the afternoon, a rising curiosity accompanied the return home to investigate the busy signal problem. Will the phone company have to be called in to fix it?

Upon arriving home and opening the door, a clue became immediately apparent. Both phone extension cords were seen leading away from the kitchen, snaking down the hallway in two black parallel lines, disappearing under the closed door of Eldest Daughter's bedroom.

BOB WILKINSON

The normal courtesy of "knock first before entering" a child's room was unceremoniously set aside by executive decision. Upon opening the door, the view that greeted the eye was of Eldest Daughter reclining on her bed with a phone glued to each ear, totally absorbed by joyous giggling, as she engaged in simultaneous conversations with two people. I am sure she felt that finally her parents had established good communications for her!

February 2006

SEPIA-TONED ARCHIVES

BOB WILKINSON

In Custody of an Uncertain Future

My Window View of Family Life

A shadow flashed by the window, causing my eye to wander from the closely-typed pages on my desk; it was followed by a series of bird-like cries. Although tempted to rise from my chair to discover the shadow's source, I dutifully returned to my review of the court report, due in Juvenile Court the next day. I cut a deal with my curiosity to postpone looking up again until after I finished with the report. I re-read the social worker's final draft of a description of the family's neglect of their two children, which included interviews with teachers about their shabby and undernourished condition when they attended school, which was haphazard at best. The psychologist's report about the older child was attached, along with the psychiatric evaluation of the mother, but, breaking my promise to my conscience, I yielded instead to my curiosity about the world outside my window before finishing it.

The view from the window of Children's Protective Services' second story prominence onto the roof surface below exposed a wall projected upward to one side. Against the comer, in a crevice formed by the vertical and horizontal surfaces, poised a small hawk with something in its beak. After a moment, it bent down and, to my surprise, delivered it to two small nestlings I hadn't seen until then. After that, its mission apparently complete, the hawk flew off as another bird, slightly larger, circled overhead, its cry of *killy, killy* similar to the sound I had heard earlier. It was unmistakable; it was a Kestrel and probably the mate of the hawk which had just left.

I was at that moment interrupted by the sound of a more human voice.

"Do you have any questions about my court report?" The question brought my attention back to my neglected task. I quickly read the psychologist's report and the psychiatric evaluation, signed the report, and gave it to Ruth, the waiting social worker who hurried off, no doubt offended by my puzzling window gazing, a distraction from what she could rightfully consider an urgent responsibility. After all, it would be she who would be on the spot, presenting the department's plan for the children to the judge in consultation with the children's attorney.

With Ruth gone, I felt it safe to return to the window to check on the status of my avian family. Within moments, one of the Kestrels returned to its chicks with a meal in its bill, clearly a mouse, and stuffed it into the gaping bill of one of the chicks. Again, my attention was distracted, this time by my secretary Mary, who brought another court report. She informed me that Janice, a social worker in my emergency response unit, had just called in to say that she would be late for her conference because her meeting with a police officer and emergency room physician about the medical examination of an abused youngster reported this morning was taking longer than expected.

1 turned back from the window to concentrate on the next reading task, a shorter one fortunately. It was a petition outlining the reasons, to be given at a detention hearing, to keep in emergency care, pending a full investigation, a fourteen-year-old girl sexually abused by her mother's boyfriend. This was a horrifyingly routine matter in my line of work. I knew from my secretary's message that I would soon have some unplanned free minutes at my disposal to return to the window. If I omitted a trip to the coffee shop with a co-worker, I could save some more time for nest surveillance. After all, it is not every day when the routine of responding to the abuse of humans towards their children is interrupted by a family of birds diligently raising their young.

May 2012

SEPIA-TONED ARCHIVES

The Lost And Not Always Found Department

In the San Mateo County Children's Protective Services Emergency Response Unit it was sometimes an uneventful morning when I came in to the office, the kind of morning which might allow time to catch up a little on the uncompleted work of the day before. However, there were mornings when the harvest of the previous night's referrals or admissions to emergency foster care meant immediate attention, whether or not all brain cells were in good working order, or whether there had been time for a cup of coffee to sweep away the morning cobwebs. Monday mornings were particularly vulnerable to surprises. One such morning brought the news of a "found object," as described by police, a toddler who had been picked up alone and deserted on Skyline Blvd. near Highway 92 by a deputy, after a passing motorist had alerted the Sheriff's office.

The child's name, age, address, and parental identity were unknown; it was a girl, that much was known. The initial police report was skimpy with details, reflecting the mystery of the event and the meagerness of starting points for the social worker who would be assigned to the case. Fortunately, the Sheriff's office did not close out their case, but pursued it as a missing person or persons, in an attempt to locate parents or relatives. It drew the attention of the press, which in turn brought many offers of adoption, and questionable claims of relationships to the child.

Police investigation eventually sorted it out and produced an identity for the child and her missing mother, whose home was miles from the spot where the child was found. A neighbor was even able to name a grandmother living on a Caribbean island. No trace of the mother or the father ever appeared during the several months the county had custody of the child, and eventually, with the assistance of the American Embassy on that Caribbean Island nation and a local social agency there, the maternal grandmother was approved as a potential home. The youngster, in the company of a staff member, was finally flown to be with her.

BOB WILKINSON

With the passage now of more than three decades, it is possible that the mother has been located, or we could conjecture that the child, now an adult, might have returned to this country to conduct her own inquiries. In any case, although the child's long-term future lay beyond the scope of our responsibilities, it was not beyond our interest or imagination.

On another day late in 1978 after, in the words of the German American novelist Ursula Egli, "the night was shaken and this was what fell out" sort of morning, a "found object" was turned over to us. Because the child was found at the San Francisco Airport, which is located in San Mateo County, this ten-year-old girl ended up in our custody. Her name was known, as were her previous whereabouts, but her future was unclear. She was one of very few living Jonestown orphans, one who survived that well-publicized mass suicide/massacre in Guyana, but whose parents had not.

Flown here a week or so after the tragedy, she bore the physical marks of a failed attempt to kill her—a bandaged knife wound on her neck. This child came accompanied by a modest amount of information, but included the warning from police that her location must be kept strictly confidential to protect her from possible additional harm. It was not known whether there might be someone around interested in disposing of her as a potential witness, since one attempt had already been made.

We were to learn later how most of the few who escaped the Jonestown poisoned Kool-Aid, or who attempted to run away into the surrounding jungle, were hunted down by the armed enforcers at Jonestown. Congressman Leo Ryan, who represented our district, was assassinated during the Jonestown massacre on November 18, 1978. His attempts at an investigation into Jonestown apparently triggered the tragedy. His assistant Jackie Speier was severely wounded—shot five times, and waited twenty-two hours before help arrived—but survived. She later became a congresswoman representing much of the political territory that Ryan had represented.

To maintain security, the girl would not be enrolled in school, nor would her location appear on the Department's internal daily roster of children in emergency care. The first appointment for her would be with the pediatrician at the county hospital to determine the extent of injury and treatment for the knife wound. Settling on her future home would be our goal. Assessing whether there were relatives who could care for her in safety would be the primary task. The decision, approved in juvenile court, was to place her with a relative in another county and to transfer court jurisdiction to that county.

Dealing with the long-term consequences of the child's close brush with death, and the traumatic loss of her parents, lay beyond our temporary goals. Still, in recalling that girl or remembering Jonestown, it would always be a question that we would wonder about, but had no power to answer or to influence. Her neck wound would certainly heal, but her future mental health and emotional well-being after such catastrophic events in her young life was not something we could secure for her, although it would obviously be a concern as she matured. We could not find a certainty of future happiness or security for her; that responsibility would have to be entrusted to others, not the so-called "lost and found."

July 2012

BOB WILKINSON

To Usher in Bursts of Bluebirds

SEPIA-TONED ARCHIVES

In the Bird Nests of My Mind

Black ravens have lately come to roost in my cranium,
Croaking dire warnings, flapping alarm wings,
Calling up dark thunderheads to rumble in my mind.

Where went my swifts and swallows snatching winged witticisms
from azure skies to feed hope-hungry mouths deep in my brain cells?

Or darting kingfishers, plucking shiny, swimming reassurances
from the crowded cataracts below,
nurturing their naive young in the synapses of my consciousness?

Have those minions of misery taken long term leases
in the tenements of my noggin?

To keep away preening parrots offering crackers of comfortable
mantras
in their beaks?

Or the iridescent hummingbirds in electric motion,
Dancing among fragrant nectars of desire?

Where are the hoots of owls hunting out the furtive rodents of
rusty lamentations?

Who is to rid my crowded mental aviary
of its smoke-blackened squatters,
leaving their reeking calling cards of partly digested gloom?

Could their unwilling host with medical elixirs evict them?
Or merely mask their shadows with rivers of rum?

BOB WILKINSON

Or, better, hope that the return of the tender close embrace
of a familiar feathery roost
Decked with crimson-edged feathers and Mozart memories
Dancing Dowitchers and crowing cormorants
Send them scurrying forever from my burdened rafters?

To usher in bursts of bluebirds
With cheerful warblers and choirs of curlews
To cleanse and perfume the chambers of my psyche,
And weave strands of affection with strips of laughter
To mend the mold and rot in the nests of my mind

March 2006

Poetry Penance

April is National Poetry Month, but there has been little in the press to draw attention to it, other than an article about a poet in Ukraine named Dr. Boris Khersonsky. A psychiatrist who uses social media to try to heal his country, he conveyed poems and essays urging his countrymen, for their own sake, to recognize and admire their differences in their national identity make-up. It reminded me of another much celebrated Ukrainian poet of almost two centuries ago, Taras Shevchenko, whose memorial building looks out imposingly over the Dnieper River from its west bank south of Kiev.

In our country, some poetry advocates urge us to observe the month by keeping a poem in our pocket which we should whip out and recite to anyone we happen to meet. This is the story of someone who tried that, and spent thirty days observing poetry month in a way not anticipated.

One fine spring day, Ned was driving his red Toyota convertible with the top down, enjoying the fresh green countryside, when the sound of birds chirping and the even humming of his engine were drowned out by the scream of a siren, a motorcycle policeman coming into view in his mirror. After he pulled over to the side of the highway, he realized that he had probably not been paying much attention to the speedometer. So, in addition to presenting his license to the California Highway Patrol (CHP) officer, he also drew from his pocket a poem in hopes that it might help avoid a citation. He began as follows:

> Oh, gentleman of the law
> You're among the finest I ever saw.
> > But hear my excuse
> > Spare me the noose
> And I hope this doesn't stick in your craw.

BOB WILKINSON

The officer cut him short by also pulling out of his pocket a slip of paper, and replied:

> Since you paid no heed
> To the limit of speed.
> > You must now trudge
> > To court and face the judge,
> And then much better poetry you will need.

Later, in the courtroom the judge entered and reviewed with a frown the poetry evidence provided by the CHP officer; she asked Ned if he had anything to say in his defense. Ned stood and smiled as he spoke:

> Over your highways I did roam.
> In my head I held a poem
> > Up hills I did climb
> > Seeking words that would rhyme
> Your honor, 'tis spring, my brain is far from home.

The judge's face turned gray,
As she stood erect to say:

> Your limericks stink
> Flush them down the sink
> Instead of such trash
> Try reading Ogden Nash
> While sitting thirty days in the clink.

Hamlet's Advice to Writers

"Get thee to a nunnery!" Hamlet's words of dismissal to Ophelia might have been good advice if he were thinking of her as an aspiring writer, or I suppose, if he were speaking to me: "Get thee to a monk's cell." If I had done so, I might have accomplished something by the likelihood of keeping distractions to a minimum, whether with my sculpture tools or my keyboard.

Twenty years ago, I thought that I could concentrate much better in a sculpture studio than I could at home, where everything could claim my attention, from the telephone, to noticing that the paint was peeling from the house trim. A room of his own! That was to be the answer. I could chip away happily at the apricot log that I had retrieved from an orchard in Brentwood, and not raise my eyes from my workbench until lunch time; at least, that was the theory. However, sanding a four-foot length of wood for a week can become as exciting as painting the side of the house, so the first person who unsuspectedly walked past my door might be intercepted to pass the time of day. The fly that buzzes past my head must be pursued. Coffee time! A break for a cuppa can easily distract me until time for lunch.

In a different medium—writing—the theory was that if I worked early enough in the morning, shut off in the room with the computer, I could escape the pull of chores and temptations of the world at large, like vacuuming the lint-strewn rug or reading the morning paper. Diversion can sometimes come abruptly, however, when typing an overly enthusiastic phrase or exclamation mark causes my elbow to knock a cup of hot green tea into my lap.

Cleaning up after a work session with chisel or keyboard requires different chores. Tidying up after a session of messy writing means hard work. I might have to sweep unused metaphors into the recycling bin, adverbs into the garbage pail, and clichés into the toxic refuse pail, and set aside unused single letters to be used on the next grocery list. I search the carpet in vain to reclaim some precious punctuation marks, particularly periods, as I do not have enough of them, so my sentences are in danger of running on until sunset, or until I am gasping for breath.

With my studio, it means raking together wood chips, on a good day scattered across my floor like sparks from a welder's torch, some to be used as mulch, others to be burned in the fireplace. But if Silicon Valley ever runs out of silicon for computer chips, my wood chips are ready to answer the call.

Now that I am planning to give up my studio, maybe I should take up a harmless hobby like butterfly collecting!

March 2014

Peace Comes to the Artist

The naked newborn wood sculpture
    can it be accepted as such?
Stands naively on my chipped and battered bench
    as if to claim in all youthful innocence
the honor, as yet unearned.

Wood chips scattered on the scarred and littered floor
    aromatic, scuffed about by worn down soles
pungent with odor of earlier doubts.

Sharp-edged chisels and ponderous mallet lie at rest
    their *pok pok* sounds of cutting and carving ended
Files' rasping sounds now silent.

Misgivings sanded away as sharp corners
    yield and bulges blend
Exhausted sandpaper creased and crumpled
    as desiccated debris underfoot.

Smooth now to the touch of calloused hands
    curves caressed and edges gently fingered.
The erotically bare walnut skin awaiting
    drops of linseed oil, the baptismal anointment
 sealing open pores, the end of labor,
    mid-wifed into an uncertain world.

Soaking thirsty surfaces, spreading the elixir
    with loving tactile strokes;
massaging the receptive wood,
    flooding every crevice and cranny.

Wax and polish, then arm sweeping
    to sweetly buff the finish.
At last, anxiety recedes

BOB WILKINSON

Critics, those shoulder-perched magpies,
    sent packing;
      Peace prevails.

January 2011

Fears I Have Known

There have been healthy fears that have helped keep us humans evolutionarily successful through the ages, I suppose, like fear of snakes and saber-tooth tigers. I have had some fears that may have kept me safe from their more modern equivalents, like my sixth grade teacher, whose frowning look could make me feel like crawling into the desk inkwell. A few years later, my high school teacher's command to come to the front of the class and write a solution to a trigonometry problem on the blackboard could cause me to search for a hidden trapdoor that I could mercifully disappear through.

Then there was my basic training drill sergeant at that godforsaken spot, just south of Oklahoma, who delighted in making us stand at attention for hours under a hot Texas sun, even if we were suffering from the effects of the mess hall food, which gave most of us diarrhea. He then took delight in sending us to Kitchen Patrol (KP) for a twelve-hour shift, thereby with contamination, adding more victims to the trots platoon. I dreaded meeting his gaze when he was contemplating those most eligible for his next assignment.

For several years after retirement, my worst occasional nightmares included some variation of the fear of discovering that I had to appear in juvenile court in ten minutes to face the judge and present a case that I knew absolutely nothing about.

A more recent source of fears has been of a slight ninety-eight-pound young woman, deceptively harmless in appearance, who I encounter every six months, my dental hygienist. She can look me straight in the eye and know the truth, detecting my dental sins without even examining my mouth. Fear of that encounter changes my lifestyle for as much as a full week before the appointment, when I search the drawer to find the dental floss.

I could mention technology terror when faced with unfamiliar messages from the Internet, or lack of response from the remote control, or those evil-ish, new, centralized, downtown parking meters, which look like a final exam in a class that I somehow missed attending.

The worst fear that I have, recalling FDR's iconic statement that the fear we have is of fear itself, is fear of artistic failure. It assumes the image of a large, black, feathered bird which comes to perch on my shoulder, its sharp feet ready to dig into my flesh, and its pointy bill ready to pinch my ear whenever I scribble out a sentence or begin carving a new sculpture. It sometimes takes me a few minutes, or even several days, to remember the right incantation to banish it in reluctant flight, a reversal of the Budweiser commercial: "This is not for you, it's only for me, you constant critic!" If uttered with conviction often enough, it acts as a spell to keep the bird a short distance away. But from a branch nearby, it keeps an alert eye on me, ready to return at the first sign of equivocation.

In summary, I acknowledge that I am but a quivering, fear-riddled, mass of ectoplasm. For analysis, a psychic biopsy taken of me should be sent, not to the psychiatric clinic, but to the Monterey Bay Aquarium, Jellyfish Division.

October 2012

SEPIA-TONED ARCHIVES

BOB WILKINSON

The Soul of My Boots

My Boots, My Soul

"These boots are made for walkin'" was a line from a 1966 Nancy Sinatra song adored at one time by my then eleven-year-old daughter. Boots made for walking have taken me from the hot sands in the depths of Death Valley to the thin air atop Mt. Whitney. I could do without them as soon as I could do without my dinnertime glass of Chardonnay.

When new, the ankle-high tops of cowhide were as smooth as a baby's bottom, and with laces taut as the sinews of a mule. They have clambered over Sierra granite and jumped over rushing creeks. They have traversed gentle slopes up to the Continental Divide, past the half hidden trapper's cabin in the Wind River Mountains of Wyoming, carrying me through many a long day of rock hopping with never a twisted ankle.

Although they have endured a number of reincarnations, from polished Army boots, to $70 hiking shoes from REI, they have retained the same persona, molded by the very same pair of feet and housing the same toes. No wonder the bottom of the boot is spoken of as the sole; I prefer an alternate spelling, as in soulmate. The tread they left on a dusty mountain trail said to the wind, "I was here." Part of my soul shall linger on this rugged, rock-strewn slope with the gnarled junipers as sentinels, their wind-sculpted branches beckoning me to ignore my straining lungs, on and on to ever higher summits.

Lacking sherpas, I trusted to my foot gear to help bear the backpack's weight, to find the trace of the trail hidden beneath a melting summer snow pack, or find the path among the trackless boulders.

Once, in Lapland, hiking without my boots, I paid the price of foot gear infidelity for trying to hike without my soul mates. In my street tennis shoes, I slipped on a wet log while photographing reindeer. As penalty for my footgear philandering, I was punished by cracked ribs and a gashed head, resulting in remorse and the swearing of ever after faithfulness to my boots.

BOB WILKINSON

If they could speak, what stories would they tell? Perhaps the terrifying encounter in open country of a Sierra lightning storm crashing around me and my companions as we sought shelter among the boulders. Perhaps the time the boots were left outdoors and, perhaps out of spite for being exiled from household warmth, they offered a home to a passing bumblebee, which stung my toe when my foot was inserted the next morning.

In recent years, the boots have developed creases—wrinkles, actually. The dull surface no longer reflects the skin-softening cosmetics used to waterproof them. Now, when resting on the floor awaiting the next trip, they list heavily to one side as though feeling the burden of their many years of faithful service. The fastenings are frayed, no longer "straight laced." The eyelets have lost their brightness, and at the toe, a gaping hole will reveal my sock and allow moisture to seep in.

The tongue has curled up, dry and arthritic. Instead of greeting me with their former eagerness for the trail, the boots only grudgingly accommodate my feet. But, like long-loved and faithful dogs, they bravely wag their collective tails and march forth when whistled to.

When passed up on the hill by younger boots, they do not behave jealously or with a testosterone-induced burst of acceleration, but assume an air of dignified indifference, too blasé to answer the challenge. Even a mother pushing a stroller on the street can pass them by now without them feeling any self-consciousness or diminishment. Like Nancy Sinatra probably, they have seen their prideful days of youthful exuberance.

December 2011

Community Markets

The odor of hot popcorn scented the air to greet me at the semi-weekly San Mateo Farmers Market, spread out on the asphalt parking area on a windy day at the College of San Mateo. The strains of a guitar-strumming musician singing with a voice that had experienced better days grated on my ears. "Very sweet, very sweet," shouted one mustachioed peach and apricot vendor, not complimenting the singer, but offering samples from behind a table overflowing with fruit. The taste of the peach slice was indeed as sweet as he proclaimed it to be, and I succumbed to the enticement.

Breads from an Indian or French bakery beckoned. At the edge of the market, behind a folding table, stood two eager signature gatherers for the latest petition promising a better future in state government. A colorfully dressed woman made clever balloon animals or hats for children. In a stall operated by a Cambodian woman, a ten-year-old daughter sold bok choy and made change for customers without recourse to a calculator. Several languages could be detected, including Spanish and Russian. Nearby a man and wife conversed in French about some details at a vendor's booth. Others who were speaking in Mandarin poked and prodded the fruit and vegetables.

Mandarin language memory associations carried me back to experiences in other lands, such as along an alley in Nanjing, one of the ancient capitols of China, where the odors and sounds were different. When live eels were purchased, they would be extracted from their tanks and promptly stripped of their skins before the customer's eyes, freshness ensured. Live chickens clucked away in small wire enclosures, available for inspection by customers. The pervasive odors of cooking noodles were tempting. The crowds jostled one another, and sometimes loud voices were exchanged as hard bargaining took place. A young man on a bicycle negotiated his way down the street with several live ducks trussed from the handle bars, heads hanging down and gently quacking.

BOB WILKINSON

In Urumqi, Xinjiang Province, the traditional early morning market got underway outside the modern, twenty-story hotel, with produce hauled in by donkey cart, wheeled in on bicycles, or with push carts. Live fish were offered fresh from a portable tank. Women squatted on the ground behind large baskets of boiled colored eggs or containers of milk and yogurt, conversing in Uighur or Kazakh. Few Han Chinese were in evidence in this part of China. In all this busy chaos, there were no signs of street musicians, social activists, or balloon ladies to amuse the children, provide entertainment, or to sell popcorn. This market was serious business; nothing frivolous intruded. No Kmart or Walgreens stores were available either.

Farther around the world at a market in the Anatolian city of Selcuk, a smiling fourteen-year-old boy sold to customers from a pan of round pastries. In Turkey, no schooling was required for children after the age of fourteen. Meanwhile, a young man strode by balancing a large tray of the pastries atop his head. At the side of the road, young boys offered to shine my shoes. I wasn't sure how my tennis shoes would look after that. Towers of unglazed pottery were displayed, while heaps of hot peppers gave a hint of the spicy Turkish cuisine. Knives were sharpened by a man operating a foot-powered grindstone. Shoes could be repaired while you shop, by a cobbler seated on a stool working with hand tools in his lap. A waiter bearing a tray of coffee and small cups issued from a nearby coffee house wended his way toward the proprietor of one of the stalls.

There was something that spoke of a more personal, human touch with all of these markets. There were no movie star magazines at the check-out counters, where electronic eyes scanned bar codes, no "paper or plastic" choices, no freezer food, or cardboard containers either. Children were often meaningfully involved in the family enterprise, waiting on customers, running errands, and safeguarding the family transport. In some cases, unfortunately, economic choices may have dictated their participation in the family business at the cost of continued school attendance.

In the community markets, I sensed feeling a step closer to the growing of food and production of household goods. While the actual planting and reaping of crops is not experienced, the killing of the animal or fish you purchase often is witnessed close up. Setting aside some of the health and safety issues, the word authenticity comes to mind. I felt some satisfaction in the small act of supporting an alternative to agribusiness, or other corporate structures, which compensated for the lack of refrigeration.

In China, hunks of meat, probably lamb, were spiked on top of the iron fence for all to inspect, including flies. Piles of purple eggplant and long green beans were sprawled on the street surface. Shirts and trousers were hawked by a young woman standing atop a cart. Nearby, the piercing sounds from traditional Chinese horn and drum players sitting on the steps of a department store announced a special sale. An air of urgency pervaded the scene, until everyone, every vestige of the daily people's market, vanished without any noticeable signal at exactly 9AM. The ancient scene was replaced by modern taxicabs and delivery vans for the hotel disgorging a few tourists or Chinese businessmen.

Farther west along the Taklamakan Desert near the Pakistan border, a weekly market scene unfolded on a Sunday (our name for the day), as it has for a reputed two thousand years, in the fabled city of Kashgar. The air was clouded with the dust of donkey carts and honking vans arriving from desert oases miles away, loaded with vegetables and merchandise such as rugs, baby cribs, pots, and pans. The soft sounds of sheep *baa*-ing mixed in with the cacaphony of human sounds as they, along with goats, were herded down the streets to an enclosure for bartering. Some of the same sheep could later be seen being butchered and skinned. Men wore the traditional Muslim cap and loose-fitting garments; women were cloaked from head to toe.

The constant cry of "posh, posh," meaning "coming through," sounded at my shoulder as men pushed through the throngs with their wagons or donkeys. The prevailing odors were a heady mixture

of barbecued lamb, steamed buns, and donkey dung. At the side of
the street, a sign showed a cut-away diagram in bright color of human
jaws, advertising in graphic, anatomical fashion that dentistry was
available. Men sat in barber's chairs at the side while the stream of
people surged by. In nearby streets, children patiently sat, minding
donkey carts while parents sold their wares in the market. Some older
children were busy fabricating aluminum pots or mending shoes. The
very young were often entrusted with errands. One example was a
pair of boys, age five, who trudged down the dusty street, trying not
to spill water from a kettle slung between them, on a wooden rod
resting on their shoulders.

Memorable Meals

Four days into our backpacking trip—our first such experience—my two friends and I were camped in Crabtree Meadows, elevation 10,000 feet, at the western foot of our ultimate destination, Mt. Whitney, which we planned to summit that day. Our meals thus far had been composed mostly of something called MPF, or multipurpose food. It closely resembled the feed I had given to our chickens at home and smelled about the same. It was before the days of commercial backpacking food with all its choices of dehydrated vegetables or stew sealed in plastic pouches. There were a few seasonings, thoughtfully provided by my friends' mother, but the monotony of the diet was beginning to take its toll on our morale. Adding lots of water to the MPF meant soup; less water meant artificial hamburger. It might pass today as basic vegan food for those seeking personal penitence, but at that time I wondered if we would pretty soon begin to cackle like chickens.

However, that morning we awoke in our sleeping bags to the sound of horses being saddled and the subdued voices of the two park rangers who had ridden into the meadow the previous evening. As soon as they saw that we were awake, one asked if we would like the trout which they caught that morning from the stream flowing through the meadow. They had just received an urgent radio message to hasten to a fire which had started the day before, presumably by lightning, and they would not have time to stay and cook the fish themselves. Neither Dave, his brother Tom, nor myself were fishermen, nor were we even equipped with fishing poles. The thought of something to eat for breakfast besides MPF brought us very fast out of our drowsy stupor. Clothed in the same jeans and shirts we had started with, and encumbered with the dust and perspiration of the trail, we were probably not the most civilized diners to enjoy a meal that we anticipated was gourmet. When a fire was built and the trout fried, it seemed like the best fish I had ever remembered tasting; it supplied the energy and mood necessary for the day's 4,000 foot climb to Mt. Whitney's peak.

BOB WILKINSON

Leaping forward about forty years to Moscow during the Gorbachev Glasnost years, my wife and I, along with our companions on our personal diplomacy trip to the Soviet Union, boarded the midnight train to Kiev, where we would embark on a riverboat headed down the Dnieper River.

"Nyet!" was the curt reply from the conductor to my inquiry about where I could find a glass of water or some food. While not a frequent train traveler, I had this naive idea that a train from the country's capital, Moscow, would be equipped with the amenities that made traveling comfortable, if not luxurious. I realized that our twelve-hour trip without prospect of food or beverage was less of a romantic movie version of train travel, like "Murder on the Orient Express" with tuxedoed waiters and silver utensils, and more reminiscent of the cattle car-like troop trains I once experienced. Other passengers, apparently Soviet, seemed either oblivious to the Spartan circumstances, or remarkably unconcerned about it.

As I complained about it with another member of the group I was traveling with, I noticed that the conductor had returned, and had unveiled a large brass samovar at the far corner of the car, filled it with water by turning a knob, and left without a word. A few minutes later, one of the Russian passengers went to the samovar, turned a tap, and filled a cup—his own—with hot, steaming tea. After others followed suit, I tried it, my wife improvising a cup from a motion sickness bag she had obtained on the Aeroflot flight a few days earlier. I couldn't imagine yet at that point in the trip what other use a barf bag could have on a train without the presence of food to make one nauseated.

While gathered around the samovar enjoying the hot beverage, we aroused the curiosity of some of the Soviets, amused by my use of the barf bag, who inquired in halting English where we were from. Learning that we were "Amerikanski," there were smiles and more questions. There was a sincere interest in and awareness of iconic American TV shows such as *The Streets of San Francisco*. Pretty soon a vodka bottle appeared. It was passed around and poured into barf bag cups, the samovar abandoned to the women Soviet passengers.

Vodka-induced conviviality was soon further enlivened by a man, introducing himself as Boris, who hauled out a balalaika from beneath his seat. He began to play Russian songs, none of which we knew, until, in apparent deference to us tourists, the melody of "Moscow Nights" rang out, an informed choice since we had practiced this old classic during our Russian lessons. "Promise me, my love, as the dawn appears, and the darkness turns to light..." It seemed appropriate.

Well, by this time, amid music and awash in vodka, I was no longer concerned about sustenance, nor did I miss the sleep that we might have tried to seek on the hard seats. So, Russian lesson number one: if you feel food deprived, try vodka.

After a while, the first light of dawn appeared at the windows. The first rays of sun revealed a glimpse of people with pails searching among the trees, perhaps to gather berries, igniting in me visions of food again. Yet six or seven more hours remained before our destination. Was I to learn Russian lesson number two? Forbearance, patience, and low expectations?

While the sun was still low in the eastern sky, the train made its first daylight stop at a very small, old and dreary-looking rural station. Scattered among those waiting to board were several babushkas carrying baskets or pushing carts, and looking upward toward our coach. When it was apparent that they were selling fruit, a few passengers raised their windows, and after a moment's discussion of prices, hauled in a handful of *yabloki*, or apples, in exchange for coins. Lacking the linguistic skills necessary for negotiation, I simply stretched out my hand with a few kopeks and hoped for the best. The apples yielded up to me in exchange by an elderly woman looked bright green, felt hard as billiard balls, and the taste? No lemon could be more sour, but who was I to be fussy in my breakfast-deprived condition? However, after the sourness had a chance to mix with the vodka consumed earlier, I momentarily regretted the loss of that converted barf bag,

The next stop produced women selling what turned out to be pears — a riper, sweeter-tasting selection. What would be next? I wondered.

This was followed by a stop where piroshkies and other pastry concoctions were sold from pushcarts. Again, my outstretched kopeks were rewarded, this time with a paper-wrapped and still warm parcel that pleased my taste buds, going a long way toward easing my hunger. In the communist-oriented economic system of 1989 there was fortunately room for small scale home-based capitalism.

As we rolled on toward Kiev, I felt that I was riding alongside cafeteria stations, a kind of movable feasting, and had come to anticipate each stop to see what new morsel might be on the menu. By the time I arrived in Kiev and we bid a sleep deprived "*Dasvidaniya!*" to our Russian railway companions, my lament about the missing dining car, or the lack of sleeping berth, had long ago been forgotten. After all, who needs a meal with tablecloth and napkins when, to paraphrase that 11th Century Persian Omar Khayyam, you have a loaf of piroshky, a jug of vodka, and song?

September 2015

From Peninsula To Perestroika

"From Peninsula to Perestroika" could describe personal diplomacy trips that I took because of my alarm about the Cold War arms race in 1987 and 1989. *Zdravstvuyte!* or hello, greeted us in Russian as we embarked on the riverboat Maxim Gorky from Rostov–on-Don to steam along the Don River and up the Volga. This was a year after a delegation of Russians had traveled with much media fanfare through America's heartland along the Mississippi River.

With the cold war, the predominant international issue during the 1980's, the accelerating nuclear arms race was spinning out of control in the view of much of the public. While the Cold War formed an organizing force for most political leaders in this country, using the fear of communism to promote military budgets or interventions in the affairs of other counties, it also sparked a national movement to curb the arms race. "Peace" campaigns came to be feared and suspect, even with opposition to the nuclear arms race becoming popularly supported, as for example, the Nuclear Freeze campaign. Fear of dissent and of political backlash affected schools and institutions. For instance, a high school principal in San Mateo forbid a student group to organize if it included that "unpatriotic" word, peace.

Against this background, I helped organize an all-day symposium to confront the arms race, held at the College of San Mateo in 1986. One engaging speaker, a Palo Alto activist for World Citizenship, described citizen diplomacy trips to the Soviet Union, during which ordinary people of both countries could intermingle, and in so doing, try to understand one another better. With the urging of my wife, we traveled with an organization in Connecticut to the Soviet Union the following summer when Mikhail Gorbachev was first championing Glasnost (openness) and Perestroika (restructuring) in his country.

The idea of our traveling beyond the Iron Curtain raised fears among our offspring, family, and friends who, I think, had visions of us languishing in Siberian gulags.

BOB WILKINSON

Bravely trying out our twelve lessons in Russian, I learned that sometimes a little knowledge can be hazardous. I discovered this to my chagrin when trying to convey a compliment in Russian to an older teenage member of a group who greeted us in good English. Instead of evoking the expected smile, my comment caused him to visibly blanch, leading him to complain that I had just called him simpleminded. So much for my initial foray into citizen diplomacy! I could only hope I hadn't contributed to prolonging the cold war.

Most of the time, my halting attempts at Russian led to Soviets overcoming their hesitance about their English so that we would converse in our language. But one time we met a Russian Stalingrad battle veteran who spoke no English, but could converse with my wife in German because he had spent time in a POW camp in Germany. Though Chinese from Hawaii, my wife knew some German from childhood family friends, and a youth trip to rebuild Germany after World War II, sponsored by the World Council of Churches.

It was often an embarrassment to discover not only how many people spoke better English than I did Russian, but also how much better informed they were about our country than we were about the Soviet Union. For example, one of our Russian hosts asked us to jot down all the countries we could think of which shared a border with the United Socialist Soviet Republic (USSR). The meager results were revealing. Similar ignorance prevailed when asked to name some current Russian writers. Some Soviets knew the names of our elected representatives. We discovered that Russians knew many of our writers; Mark Twain and Jack London held a special appeal. It was not uncommon to see streets named for Russian poets; rising high on the banks of the Dneiper is a prominent memorial commemorating a famous Ukranian poet, Taras Shevchenko.

Some of what people knew about us had been gleaned from TV. For instance, at the mention of San Francisco, a Russian young person referred to it as being a "dangerous" place to live, citing the TV series *The Streets of San Francisco.*

Cultural differences burst forth on such subjects as money. For example, a Russian general and his wife who shared a seat with us on the boat asked out of the blue what my income amounted to. This was not an uncommon question. In this country, we hold such personal information closely to our chests, to be shared only with our accountants, and reluctantly, with the IRS. Perhaps in their non-capitalistic society such information was much more widely known, with the disparity between the lowest and highest paid being much narrower, less diverse than in our country, as well as being unaffected by the intricacies of the marketplace.

The Russian attitude toward peace was manifested by a very different tone and level of conviction compared to the attitude among the leaders of our country at the time. This was evident as we toured the many memorials to the Great Patriotic War, as the second World War is known there, and met a number of veterans of that conflict which, we were reminded, resulted in the loss of more than 90% of those conscripted into the Russian Army. The memorials varied from the modest one in the town of Krem near Rostov, where the photos of the hundred or so young men and women lost from that village gazed down at us from the walls, to the soaring, awe-inspiring memorials of Stalingrad, and the mass graves entombing the victims of the siege of Leningrad stretching out in the distance before us.

We could occasionally watch ourselves on Russian TV, which featured the progress of our trip every night as we traveled from city to city, usually being met by large curious crowds, and often by a young woman in local dress offering the traditional round loaf of bread and bowl of salt. One guide who greeted us in Leningrad said she recognized most of us from the nightly newscast. Gorbachev referred to us in his speeches.

Although we participated in many earnest discussions, forums, and events with Soviets and fellow Americans about the need for reconciliation and understanding, one of the memories that endures was the chance encounter on a Moscow street with a middle-aged woman who ventured to ask if we were Americans. When we admitted we were, she begged us to stay where we were while she hustled away, to reappear moments later with her young grandson and a large bouquet of flowers which she bestowed upon us. Her spontaneous gesture of generosity spoke volumes about the readiness to surmount international tensions on a person-to-person level.

January 2006

SEPIA-TONED ARCHIVES

BOB WILKINSON

A River Flowing Uphill Against Gravity

The Ballad Of Tiny Tim

Tiny Tim's little cheeks are hot,
Portends another asthma attack;
No clinic will attend him,
Now money's only for Iraq.

Oh, my, where can they turn
health insurance they do lack,
"Just go to the ER," the big man said
There's money only for Iraq.

Sister Nell's ear is hurting quite bad,
There are sores upon her back,
The king says loud and clear,
Our money is only for Iraq.

Brave Tiny Tim falls and stumbles,
He cannot stay on track,
His parents grow deeper in debt,
The money is only for Iraq.

While little Nell cannot read,
The wealthy we must not tax.
Will she be left behind?
There's money only for Iraq.

Tiny Tim's holiday looks bleak,
The doors won't open, even a crack,
"Bah humbug," says old Scrooge,
My money's only for Iraq.

BOB WILKINSON

Return to Earth

Where is the "fire in the belly" that once propelled me to the barricades on behalf of prominent causes or political campaigns? Whether it was protesting the Vietnam War, the nuclear arms race and the Nuclear Test Ban movement, the buildup to the Iraq War, or the fight to keep the Endangered Species Act, I was fired up. I knew almost every step of the way, almost every doorway, on marches up Market Street in San Francisco to the Civic Center, or even beyond to Golden Gate Park, along with the usual cast of thousands, sometimes accompanied by a line of black-booted police on either side of the street dogging our steps for weary blocks, while press or police helicopters flapped overhead. I can remember the pride and thrill of the vast crowds surging past, chanting the slogans, carrying the homemade placards with messages such as "The Worst Day of Peace is Better than the Best Day of War." We manned the information tables, endured the 'droning–ons' of an endless succession of speakers from the platform, until we could hear Joan Baez singing, "Where have all the flowers gone?"

Inspired as I was, I would have been an easy recruit for the Paris mob storming the Bastille.

But to return to that old folk song, "Where have all the soldiers gone? Gone to graveyards, everyone." The strident sounds of trumpet calls to action now die away unanswered, fervent letters to the editor unwritten, chilly candlelight vigils not joined, and wind buffeted demonstrations unattended. No longer do I carry the placards; instead, the earth before me bears up commercially produced yard signs with messages like "Joe Smith for Supervisor" or the School Board. No more the company of foot-sore campaigners sinking wearily onto a Bay Area Rapid Transit (BART) train seat after the march. The Bastille stands un-assailed; only by occasionally peering through the mists of memory can its ramparts be glimpsed again.

SEPIA-TONED ARCHIVES

My belly fire smolders and turns to embers as my feet grow more rooted to the solid, passive earth. Yes, the earth. It takes a thousand years to build just one inch of soil with the help of compost and worms, so there's a worthy campaign I can endorse comfortably from my garden bench without putting on my marching shoes: "Support global worming."

February 2011

BOB WILKINSON

The Power of Stories, Remembering John Hersey

Like the dark background music in a tragic film or opera, the fear of death by nuclear warfare lurked during the Cold War years. This was especially true with the doctrine of MAD, or Mutual Assured Destruction, as official policy. Children were drilled in "duck and cover" exercises in classrooms, as though that would protect them. A child in my wife's first grade class, perhaps like many children at that time affected by the atmosphere of the nuclear threat, drew a picture with the caption, "*When* the bomb drops..."; he did not say *if*.

John Hersey, the author of over twenty books, including *A Bell For Adano*, wrote an account of the effects of the August 6, 1945 Hiroshima attack as told through the stories of six survivors, published in *The New Yorker* on August 31, 1946. Nearly forty years farther on in the survivors' stories, he published a follow-up entitled "Hiroshima: The Aftermath" in *The New Yorker* on July 15, 1985. Before reading it in the mid 1980's, the nuclear bomb seemed an existential threat to me, but something I felt clueless to do anything about and handled emotionally primarily through denial. Building a bomb shelter did not seem like a helpful or constructive response to the problem.

However, reading Hersey's story of Hiroshima stripped away my denial mechanism. The journalistically written account told of the effects of the blast on Hiroshima residents, their suffering from injuries, burns, and radiation. It described the loss for a time of nearly every vestige of civilization, including the loss of nine-tenths of doctors and nurses who might have helped survivors. It affected me in a way that I became like a plowed field ready for corn kernels to be dropped into its furrows. So, when I learned about an anti-nuclear group that would be meeting in San Mateo in the 1980's, I quickly agreed to attend, if for no other reason than to discover what others had in mind.

The action of the small San Mateo group was at first small potatoes. In the beginning, it was not well coordinated, confined to activities like signing petitions, for example against nuclear testing. Gradually, however, it acted as a center of gravity, drawing in hundreds of people with similar concerns. There is something to be said about taking action in the company of others, no matter how small the effort, to help counteract the feeling of helplessness in the face of what feels like an apocalyptic future. Eventually, the group adopted a more generic approach to reducing the dangers of nuclear war, very much as had Toshiko Sasaki, one of Hersey's Hiroshima survivors—that the way to prevent death by nuclear bombs was not so much to focus on the instruments of war, but to reduce the chances of conflict in general.

Returning to Hersey's Hiroshima—a tale if told only by statistics, staggering though they were—was better grasped by storytelling, the personal accounts of six survivors. It was somewhat analogous to grasping the tragedy of the Holocaust through the diary of one person, Anne Frank. As the writer Graham Swift once said, "Man is the storytelling animal." I am that animal.

November 2013

BOB WILKINSON

Persuasion: A Tale Told in Two Cities

My persuasive skills were tested to the extreme in trying to change the legislative direction of a congressman who at one time represented the district I live in. Letters typed with an actual typewriter on good stationery during the years we may designate as BC—that is, of course, Before Computer—and delivered by the postal service in Washington, were acknowledged by the congressman in the same thoughtful way each time:

"Thank you for contacting me. I appreciate your views on the matter, and when it comes before Congress, I will take your comments into consideration."

The wording of the letter seldom varied, whether my subject was about the nuclear arms race, the Cold War, a hot war, or environmental issues. The congressman was consistent. Occasionally, I would receive in the mail an unsolicited copy of remarks that he had delivered for the Congressional Record, whether or not it was related to the subjects I had written about.

In 2002, when the staccato sounds of war preparations streamed out from Washington, D.C. in an ever-increasing fusillade, peace groups here on the Peninsula, around Northern California, and across the country stirred into action, drawing to them even some heretofore passive and silent voices. Angry because of the prospect of sending men and women their age, their children's age, their grandchildren's age, they marched, they sang. They paraded with homemade signs with such slogans as, "Diplomacy, not bombs!" or "The worst day of diplomacy is better than the best day of war!" Seminars on how to write your congressional representative stressed conciseness, singleness of message, and frequency.

Petitions were signed; protests were mounted; meetings with congressmen were requested. After speeches were made in the Senate by Robert Byrd and in the House of Representatives by Barbara Lee, excerpts were sent to the congressman. Cited were predictions by prominent economists that the ultimate cost of a war would exceed one and a half trillion dollars.

The congressman who proclaimed in a candidates forum that "Iraqis would be dancing in the streets" to welcome American liberators, remained unpersuaded and unrepentant to the end, the last vote being cast against him by the Grim Reaper, who claimed him while he was still in office.

In contrast, a city on the opposite side of the globe became the focus for persuasion of a different sort. Tokyo was the home base of Kumagai Gumi, Japan's largest international construction corporation and owner of a large parcel of wetlands known as Bair Island in Redwood City. A local developer had been hired by the company to push for approval of a housing development to be known as "South Shores," almost the equivalent of another Foster City.

These wetlands, the nurseries of the Bay, sometimes referred to as its lungs and kidneys, had long been in the sights of environmental organizations hoping to reverse the long-term trend of the fill-and-build dynamic. Their goal was to preserve and restore the wetlands to their previous natural state, providing marshland for such endangered species as the California clapper rail and the salt marsh harvest mouse. Offers to buy the land had been made by POST, the Peninsula Open Space District, but all such attempts had been rebuffed, despite the serious seismic questions that would inevitably be raised if plans for development were carried forward.

Enter the National Audubon Society, which recognized the significance of the land for birdlife. A publicist with a known track record was hired to conduct a campaign to alter the equation. He consulted a retired University of Southern California (USC) professor who was knowledgeable about Japanese businesses and their culture. The subsequent action plan presented to local environmental groups at a potluck dinner in late September 1996 was to purchase full page ads in the Tokyo press and the New York Times. The goal was to embarrass the company by describing its behavior in the past as that of a "cold and distant corporation," but which could be instead transformed, and cause it to be heralded as that of an environmental hero, if it decided to preserve the land. Simultaneously, a press conference would be held at Bair Island for Japanese TV networks. To be mentioned to the press was the significance of Japanese airline passengers being able to recognize the site below while on final approach to the San Francisco Airport. Japanese environmental organizations were to be listed, whether or not they had ever heard of Bair Island. Readers were to be encouraged to contact the company to urge it to take the environmentally generous step and accept a fair market price for the land.

Within days of the appearance of the newspaper ads, the company initiated negotiations with POST to sell the land, with the plan to later transfer it to the Don Edwards National Wildlife Refuge in the Bay. The National Audubon Society President flew out to hold a televised news conference on site to thank the company and celebrate the future prospects for restoration of the wetlands.

The outcome of the two attempts at persuasion in Washington and in Tokyo could not be more different. Even though their targets and goals were dissimilar, they bear some comparison. With the representative in Washington, it was like a cloud of tiny gnats swarming in the target's face, which could be ignored or brushed aside. In Tokyo it was as though a finely machined and highly polished brass key was inserted into the target's padlock and turned with the confident twist of a practiced wrist.

March 2010

Bumper Stickers Revisited

A bumper sticker that I see frequently never fails to arouse a question. It reads, "I Brake For Pedestrians." Is it incomplete? Maybe the complete sign would read "All Others Beware!"

"Baby Onboard" is another sign that I wonder about. Is the baby a student driver?

"Keep Tahoe Blue" is a sign that I consider politically inspired, meaning Keep it Democratic.

During the run-up to, and during, the Iraq war, there were some memorable messages, either on bumpers or on signs held by marchers: "Power to the Peaceful." "Arrogance and Hypocrisy equals Disaster." "If we wanted Neanderthals, we would have elected them." "Patriotism Means No Questions." And of course, the ever popular "No War For Oil."

The hubbub in Congress about France's failure to march in lockstep with the US caused French Fries to be bad-mouthed by legislators and elicited the oppositional sign, "I Like My Fries French." One mimicked the Axis of Evil slogan with the words, "The Real Axle of Evil," showing the image of a vehicle with the then-President and Vice President as riders. Then there were the messages that were more direct and shaded on the obscene: "Impeach That Son of a Bush."

Jonathan Swift, the 17th century Irish satirist and writer, was quoted by one sign reading, "War—The Child of Pride."

It wasn't only people and cars with signs; a dog was seen with a peace sticker on his bum reading "War is Terror," and another reading "Canines against Land Mines." Baby strollers carried their own messages pasted where there could be a bumper: "War is Bad for Children and other Living Things."

BOB WILKINSON

Sometimes bumper stickers have unintended consequences; I once had a message related to peace on my rear bumper that may have inspired more violence than peace. I have wondered whether it had anything to do with my car being selected as the target of a BB gunner shooting from a passing vehicle and blowing out my rear window. Also, a friend's car was ticketed by police after he had affixed a peace slogan on his bumper. He acknowledged that his car was probably illegally parked partially across the sidewalk, but he had always done that without consequences until the peace message appeared.

I have grown weary of some bumper stickers like the one that reads "My Child is an Honor Student at Madison School." I am tempted to have my own version printed up, "My Child is an Honor Prisoner at San Quentin."

October 2013

Presidential Signing

NEWS ITEM: President Bush determines, when signing Congressional bills, a presidential finding by which he selects provisions he will observe and put into effect and which he will not. By doing this about 800 times, according to the American Bar Association, he has thus avoided, except in one instance, any veto of legislation.

Our chief executive is considered by some to be a role model; using his bully pulpit, he offers a precedent to follow in the mundane, everyday challenges of life. Why not seize on our leader's bold example and bravely push aside some of those bothersome laws and regulations which are clearly contrary to our best interests.

Inspired by our President, I have a few gripes about some senseless congressional, legislative, regulatory, or natural laws, the consequences of which I am sure were not intended and which I will cheerfully ignore as not being in my interests:

1)   Stop signs and those nauseatingly red traffic signals on my way home are a nuisance. It's OK to keep them on the side streets; placed there they may cause others to stop and thereby help speed my journey. Having to stop unnecessarily at traffic signals is clearly a waste of expensive gas and only increases our dependence on foreign oil. Burning excess fuel also contributes to global climate change, an unforgivable sin against the environment. Ignore those signs!

2)   Income taxes and elections: If our leader wants to promote democracy throughout the world, what better example of democracy practiced by his faithful constituents at home than for us to submit income taxes based only on those programs we approve of. It would be an excellent way for the government to sense the public pulse without going through focus groups or those bothersome elections. Since the military budget for present and past wars amounts to nearly half of the budget, counting interest, I can see immediately how to finance a champagne-enhanced trip to Paris. *Au revoir mes amis!*

3)   As another example, I would like to repeal the laws of gravity on those occasions when I sense that I am losing my balance and falling off the ladder. There is absolutely no sense in the utter despotism of the rule of gravity; it might even be unconstitutional. My wife's precious vase should also have been exempted before that gravitational event leading to its ignominious consignment to the dust bin.

4)   One of Newton's laws of motion is another candidate for a presidential finding: "A body at rest tends to remain at rest" was the way my high school physics teacher phrased it when lecturing on the basic laws governing the universe. Well, there are times when I would like to get my body moving from the restful position it occupies in bed, but can't because of its apparent deep reverence for that troublesome law of physics. Beware, Isaac Newton! I have my executive pen in hand!

SEPIA-TONED ARCHIVES

A National Event in San Francisco

The scene at the Daly City BART Station on a breezy, clear October Saturday morning was almost festive, as my carload of friends and I arriving from San Mateo were greeted by the sight of hundreds of people in lines that snaked for a block or more outside the station turnstiles. Almost everyone carried a sign. There were children, adolescents, great grandparents, and parents with infants in backpacks—a rainbow of color, age, and gender. Friends waved or hugged as they caught sight of one another.

Signs and banners gave witness to the diversity of organizations represented: faith groups, labor organizations, and campus groups.

The prospect of the crowds getting through the gates appeared likely to be a lengthy, almost interminable wait until, with a cheerful roar erupting from the head of the line, it was proclaimed by a ticket agent that everyone would be allowed through the opened gates without needing a ticket. The line then moved briskly and gaily forward through the flung-open barrier, surging up the escalator and onto the crowded platform above, amid happy chanter and banter, everyone relieved to be on the move. Baby strollers were wheeled into waiting positions while the track was scanned for signs of the next approaching train. This stream of humanity looked forward to soon joining the anticipated human river in San Francisco.

Homemade signs abounded, mixed with professionally printed ones. Some of the slogans were repetitious, some bore original phrases or graphics, but all with the same overarching message: peace not war. "Wake up and Smell the Coffins," said one. "Furthermore, Iraq Sunk the Maine in the Gulf of Tonkin," read another. One sign emblazoned with French and German flags said, "Thank you Old Europe." A young girl wearing a baseball cap held a sign saying simply, "Third Graders for Peace."

Earlier anxiety about the event's prospects for success melted away with the realization of the immensity of the gathering crowd. Relief also strengthened the feeling that this tide of humanity would not allow the protest to be marginalized by the press or intimidated by political leaders in Washington, at least not here. People felt they would count for something and the world would soon know it. Memories of the huge marches against the Vietnam War undoubtedly were recalled by those who had participated in them. The difference this time would be that the demonstrations would begin *before* the war. When the first ten-car train came to a stop, the crowd quickly filed in, and the vanguard of the Peninsula contingent of the great Peace March of October 2002 was on its way.

Arriving in San Francisco, the crowded train disgorged its passengers, who streamed through the station and up the escalator like a river flowing uphill against gravity, to empty out into an ocean of immense, noisy crowds on all sides. Market Street was filled from wall to wall as far as the eye could see, which actually wasn't very far unless one were an exceptionally tall person.

A cameraman watching the procession from a stationary position on the Market Street sidewalk needed two-and-a-half hours to witness the entire parade of wind-whipped banners and signs pass by on its way to Civic Center. There was a growing confidence in the power of numbers, buoyed by the speakers from the rostrum. It was fueled by reports of large crowds in other cities, which contributed to the feeling that the momentum for a peaceful resolution would have to prevail in this crisis. Of course it did not. Political leaders were unswayed, except for those few whose stands against the coming war, such as Senator Robert Byrd and Congresswoman Barbara Lee, were honored and celebrated.

Other marches occurred in the months ahead, accompanied with a sense of growing anger and despair as the participants realized that their opinions carried little weight. The war commenced despite much condemnation around the world. Was there a point to the marches and demonstrations? What good did it do? Was it just group therapy? An exercise in self-delusion? A feel-good moment? Did the failure of the movement to prevent war justify withdrawing in a defeatist surrender to the power of our national leaders? Or did it serve notice that a peace movement was alive and might portend a future trend? For every marcher were there many sympathizers who agreed with its aims?

Answers to these questions, as applied to other vigils and protests against war and injustice, have occupied the thoughts and feelings of many activists. It may be easier for them to feel some vindication now, as the tide of public opinion turns against the war, with the revelation of its cost in human life and national treasure, the country's vilification internationally with disclosures of torture and secret gulags in Eastern Europe, and the allegations that intelligence quoted by the President was biased. However, in earlier months of the war, it was not easy to find reassuring answers to these questions. Elements of the press and TV media prominently broadcast and printed political leaders' views promoting the conflict and condemning protesters as unpatriotic, even terroristic. What will history say ten or thirty years from now about the marchers who gathered that day on Market Street?

Nov. 11, 2005

Turn a Cold Shoulder, Try to Act Bolder

In Pursuit of Pleasure

My nagging Conscience Crow demands good deeds,
Like pulling those weeds before they cast seeds.

The yard is brimming with shrubs needing trimming,
and that oak tree that I should be limbing.

Oh, what a sight, on my desk letters to write,
Overdue bills, shouldn't I feel contrite?

Paint on the window sill is flaking,
My duties, those chores am I forsaking?

I'll turn a cold shoulder, and try to act bolder,
without any sorrow; can't I do them tomorrow?

How often do the Giants deserve watching,
With Tim Lincecum post season pitching?

But there again at my rose-colored window
My conscience peers in, that stern black crow!

The food encrusted plates, the leaf strewn walk,
It keeps saying, "You and I should talk"

"Get away hence, you old dark fowl!
May my conscience throw in the towel!"

So, with a Bud in hand, I turn on the TV,
To sit with pleasure, some baseball to see.

But wait, there's an error,
Not by a baseman, oh what terror!

It was Thursday, not today!
It has already happened—yesterday!

BOB WILKINSON

From outside the window, a croak-like laugh,
Pleasure denied, is that my epitaph?

October 2010

Cookbooking Through Life

How much insight into a person's life can be gleaned from a glimpse of their shelf of cookbooks? Would it reveal one's personal Gestalt? Do famous writers include their cookbooks as part of their papers to be archived by their favorite university? Those are some of the questions I emerge with after recently taking inventory of our cookbooks.

I am currently in an active downsizing crusade, filling bags with old clothing, and reluctantly at first, excess books to be donated to charity. It seemed to me that an inventory of books would be useful before deciding on their fate. This may be mostly a delaying strategy to avoid as long as possible the difficult task of sorting: this one to the city library; that one, a gift that would be disloyal to give away; this one I cannot bear to part with; I have always intended to read it since it was acquired twenty-five years ago, etc. After half an hour of trying to make decisions about which books might make the first cut, but with little progress, it was time for a recess to the kitchen for a restorative cup of green tea. It was then, with some dismay, that I caught sight of those too-often victims of benign neglect, our helter skelter rows of cookbooks.

The first that caught my eye was *A Child's Cookbook*. Each step in the preparation of a recipe is accompanied by pen and ink illustrations, probably just my level of reading comprehension. If a piece of celery is required, it is illustrated to help one identify it. I'm even reminded to wash my hands ahead of time.

For those of us who are averse to shopping for food in preparation, there is our *Edible Wild Plants of California*. Very little cooking required, it tells me. I can simply graze on native plants like miners lettuce and prepare nettle soup. The author acknowledges the stinging threat of the nettles, but offers the hopeful reassurance that the stinging doesn't last long.

BOB WILKINSON

Next to it was *The Cemetery Cookbook*, probably not a market-tested title for a bestseller. Perhaps warnings on the recipes would be in order. One might expect to find recipes with high cholesterol content or a caution to "Ask your doctor if arsenic is right for you." One recipe includes the word "ghost" in the title.

On a more restorative note, it was soon followed by *Eating for Life,* then *Meals for One,* reminiscent of a dark period in my life of bachelor culinary subsistence, with such bleakly unimaginative recipes as hamburger. After that, came the well-named *Joy of Cooking,* a battered 1946 edition, its crumbling pages held together with tape, given to me ages ago by my sister Martha, with the hopeful, but ambiguous, inscription that it might "help me make some girl a good wife." Fortunately, that volume was not long afterwards joined in the bonds of kitchen matrimony by two books with a Hawaiian accent, reflecting the cultural background of my bride—*The Pupu Cookbook,* and one titled *Wiki Wiki Kau Kau.* It had to be patiently explained to an uninitiated *haole* like me by my *kamaaina* wife that *pu pus* are island hors d'oeuvres, and *wiki wiki kau kau* means quick food. With the generous hospitality of her relatives, my culinary vocabulary soon expanded to include such luau delights as *lomi lomi* salmon and *haupia,* a completely foreign experience for someone raised by a mother who considered herself a faithful member of the English diaspora, with her dedication to such food as plum puddings, roast beef, and overcooked string beans.

Among the gift cookbooks that may have reflected my oldest son's hopes for his father's enlightenment is *The Saucier's Apprentice,* a volume intended to instill patience in the pursuit of purity with its instruction for a simple, two-day commitment of time to prepare a fine French sauce. It recommends that it would be best to select a rainy weekend, along with a novel to read. It suggests *Fanny Hill,* while keeping watch on the boiling pot, and the simple requirement that one must start with twenty-five pounds of beef and lamb bones. I am still waiting for that rainy weekend.

On the shelf mixed in with the books of time-consuming recipes to enhance the repertoire of the accomplished chef are a half dozen or so take-out menus from local Chinese restaurants, kind of a pressure release valve for the cook who is overtaxed by coming across such words as ceviche, gateau, or caponata.

Among books acquired some decades ago, was an inexpensively produced booklet on the shelf: *How to Cook Reagan's Goose,* with the subtitle *Serving up Democratic Delectables and Republican Inedibles.* It contains recipes contributed by such political luminaries of the time as Senators Alan Cranston and Gary Hart, along with Walter Mondale and Congresswoman Pat Schroeder. Senator Edward Kennedy submitted a recipe for Breadline Pudding with an appropriate political quote about Reagan budget priorities at the bottom of the page. As a political polemic, the booklet doesn't fail to remind readers that the Reagan administration famously said that ketchup is a vegetable, when allocating funds for school lunches. It lists various items for a Reagan menu, such as Food Stamp Soufflé, Welfare Relish, Poverty Popovers, and Reagan Punch.

The passage of time is marked on the shelf by the addition of sensible, health-promoting volumes such as *Cooking for the Healthy Heart* and *The Low Cholesterol Cookbook.* They have yet to be opened. Instead, there is the much thumbed *Mastering the Art of French Cooking,* with recipes that call for lots of butter and eggs. As Julia Child said, "*Toujours bon appétit!*" Until I took a look at this book a few years ago, I wouldn't have known what a quiche was if it had bit me on the lip.

So, there is my personal profile, my autobiography laid bare, a tale told by cookbooks, or my alternative to a Rorschach, and, contrary to my earlier ambition, none of the cookbooks have ended up in the discard bin.

August 2015

BOB WILKINSON

Other Worlds

With the imminent arrival of Halloween, I am inclined to acknowledge that my house is haunted; there can be no other explanation. The annual October census of other worldly inhabitants leaves little doubt that my home fairly vibrates with the ghostly antics of various species of poltergeists.

An inventory would have to begin with the presence of the well-known and unwelcome Computer Bug, a creature that lives within my electronic device that I have been seduced into using instead of the typewriter. I think that it is in fact the spirit of the Royal typewriter, long since consigned to the back of the closet, its ghost surfacing frequently enough to remind of what it considers my betrayal. I know that the Bug is a member of a large, far-flung clan, which on a moonless night celebrates together their little subversions over their human victims. In fact, a sculptor friend of mine has tried to give it some earthly form, of which I have a copy. Perhaps I should put garlic cloves around it to ward off its powers, or light candles to assuage it.

A second spectral inhabitant is the never seen, but always near, lurking ghost commonly known as the house key hider, or to give it its due, the scientifically classified *keyus obscurus*. No attempted trip away from home is without its satanic influence. It threatens to make me a recluse because of its effectiveness in putting the key in a location always different from the one in which I had so recently placed it.

A closely related household phantom is the stocking eater, or *sockus chewumupus*, a consumer or user of one sock of a pair. It may be a one-legged ghostly critter, always making off with only one sock at a time, never a pair. Once in a while, it will apparently tire of its selection and leave it for me to find in an infrequently searched area, probably a clue that it is about to steal a different colored sock.

SEPIA-TONED ARCHIVES

I cannot fail to mention the ever-present, cold temperature-loving apparition, which turns perfectly good vegetables in the refrigerator into a gray mush, sometimes known as *lettuces moldus*. If allowed to escape the refrigerator, it might wreak havoc on the environment, turning me into black protoplasm. My compost pile loves that ghost's slimy costume. Perhaps there is a connection there.

No inventory would be complete without listing the plumbing plugger spook. Referred to in our house as the *Sinkus Stinkus*, it was probably a phantom brought into the house, concealed on the shoes of a plumber brought in for another task, a banal sort of thing like a toilet tank leak. It quietly and stealthily goes about its malevolent business, tying up our drain, causing our plumber, when called to the rescue and surveying the scene, to adopt a serious, long face while writing down an estimate of the cost of repair. Exorcism of the ghost which causes this is beyond his very earthy skills. It survives any repair to strike again without so much as a groaning warning.

No wonder trick or treaters avoid our house.

October 2015

BOB WILKINSON

Drama on The Deck

A favorite spot at home, and the stage for drama starring man vs. beast, is the structure euphemistically referred to as the birdfeeder.

Ours is located in the crotch of a large, live oak tree hanging above our deck overlooking the canyon. As anyone knows who has a feeder, it is in actuality just as likely to be a free lunch distribution center for a very adaptable and determined critter, the squirrel.

In the fall, when I begin to lay out birdseed for birds, particularly the winter migrants, I observe many avian personalities. I welcome the golden-crowned sparrows, who are joined by some of the year-round species, such as the Dark-eyed Junco, and the Chestnut-backed Chickadee, which is quite tolerant of people. The Tufted Titmouse is furtive and nervous acting, seemingly fearful of spending more than a nanosecond at the feeder before flitting away. There is the Towhee and Stellar's Jay, and the Scrub Jay, which is the bully species at the feeder.

Into this mélange of bird life enters the squirrel! It confidently takes possession without a whimper from the birds, and scarfs up the seeds, stuffing them into his cheek pouches, sometimes yielding only to a more dominant, larger squirrel. In a game we always play, I run out onto the deck to scare the raider away from the feeder. The clever squirrel pauses safely and nonchalantly in the tree, beyond reach of flying missiles, returning to the feeder the moment I re-enter the house.

I have built a number of feeders with the intent of defeating the squirrels.

But how to build a successful bird feeder? I am sure this question has occupied many Nobel scientists in their labs when they might otherwise be researching a remedy for the common cold. My solution one year was to construct a contraption which could be loaded with seeds and then swung out into space to a position at least eight feet away from any tree branches or roof line. For the first several days, I gloated in proud satisfaction as I observed the birds feeding without interference from the squirrels, which could only look on with envy.

My pride was destined to be short lived, however. One morning I witnessed a squirrel poised on a tree branch which I had assumed was a safe distance away, closely eyeing the feeder, flexing his legs, doing push-ups for a while before finally launching himself into space toward the feeder. His paws barely reached the pole supporting the feeder, and he scratched and scrambled to keep from falling, eventually gaining access to the feeder. After that, his acrobatic forte was followed by several other squirrels who followed his example.

Back to the drawing board! My grudging respect for the squirrel is such that if a giant meteor should strike the earth, wiping out life as we know it, I think a squirrel would be found to have survived somewhere.

BOB WILKINSON

Voltaire

I recently read that Voltaire is credited with saying, "Words were created to hide feelings." Is there a day when we aren't either on the receiving end, or uttering some comment ourselves, or witnessing some illustration of that quotation?

I have an artist's studio, and therefore I have a collection of comments that are made to me about my art. For instance, the conversational gambit, "Tell me about that piece" could often be translated loosely as "Whatever on earth got into your head to make that?" Or, after spending time looking at my work, I may hear from someone departing, "I'll be back later to see this with my wife/husband." Strangely, the wife/husband is nowhere to be found. "You have very interesting work," said while edging toward the door, can often be interpreted as "not my style."

Dinnertime telephone calls seeking donations starting with "We so appreciate your past support" could very well mean "You cheapskate, I'm going to make you feel guilty for not contributing to this worthy cause for the last five years, and you better remove the dark blot under your name by contributing." Of course, I may use a similar smoke screen by claiming that I am just sitting down to dinner with guests and am just too busy to talk right now.

Obfuscation with language has always been with us, and is nowhere more evident than it is in politics. Any legislation that includes in its title the word "reform" you can bet is rife with ideology or special interest, whether it is Social Security or the tax code. "Healthy Forests Initiative" is a euphemism for increased logging for the timber industry. Insertion of the word "patriot" in a law that allows the government to determine what books I have checked out is intended to make us salute and keep quiet. Domestic surveillance becomes more acceptable if labeled anti-terrorism or anti-Al Qaeda to prevent another 9/11.

As the comic strip "Calvin and Hobbes" put it, "Maybe we can make language a complete impediment to understanding."

BOB WILKINSON

Stay-at-Home
Octogenarian

What Was Missing?

"There is some oatmeal on the stove, which may still be warm," was my short written note to my wife Blossom, left for her at her breakfast place in the expectation that she would soon finish dressing and come to the table. As I drove off to provide my weekly morning art lesson at a local school, I felt that I had provided at least some basic nourishment for my wife in my absence.

About an hour later, after my lesson was completed, and when starting to return home, my mind was struck suddenly by the image of the stove burner. Before I left the house, did I or didn't I turn it off? Would I find the house still standing when I got home? Would my wife be safe?

It seemed like every traffic light was red, and of course, a train chose this moment to approach, so the crossing guard was down. Another delay! As I neared home, a block away, I could see the roof! It was intact and no column of smoke was visible! No firetrucks, either. But pulling into the garage and opening the car door, I caught the unmistakable whiff of smoke.

Rushing inside, I found my wife perfectly conscious, although enveloped in a cloud of smoke, with her spoon in a bowl of com flakes.

"I turned off the oatmeal you had on the stove," she said, as I rushed to open doors and windows.

On the stove was a blackened pot inside of which was a stinking, dark mass of charcoal, no resemblance to oatmeal or anything else one could imagine on the menu.

Her next comment was more arresting. "You know, to go off and leave a stove burner on was recently listed as among the first signs of Alzheimer's."

BOB WILKINSON

Ouch! But it was not the only sign, I could painfully acknowledge, remembering my recent difficulty in finding where I had parked my car at the shopping center. What was missing this morning, though?

I could anticipate my children's looks if they got wind of this event.

"Time to turn in his license, his license to cook."

"And you mean you forgot to replace the smoke alarm battery?"

As Shakespeare's character Dogberry said in *Much Ado about Nothing,* "When the age is in, the wit is out."

But, I countered, "Didn't I get two Jeopardy questions right last night?"

"Well, anyway, Happy Chinese New Year," she said to cheer me up. Then she added, "It's the Year of the Horse."

Then it hit me. Yes, that was what was missing! What was missing was good horse sense! This could therefore be a restorative year for me—a year to absorb more horse sense.

I could almost hear my wife's unspoken admonition: "But just watch out for the oats."

February 2014

Saving Creativity

The horizontal filing system on top of my desk, otherwise known as Bob's rat's nest, is a rich trove of documents, historical and biographical, which resist being categorized adequately to fit into any of my existing organized, vertical filing folders. It continues to mount higher with every passing month, like tumbleweeds blown against a fence.

It has almost always been a comfort to cite the research which links disorder to creativity, most recently reported by researchers at the University of Minnesota and Northwestern University. Their conclusion is, "Clean spaces might be too conventional to let inspiration flow." Of course, some cynics would say it is only an excuse for laziness, that orderliness is next to moral righteousness.

I have sometimes wondered about the color of my desk. Whatever the original color, it may now be stained the color of ink, perhaps purple, from the amount of letters and various clippings, stacked inches deep, that form layers not unlike geological strata that you might meet on the side of the Grand Canyon.

Some people say they know where everything is on their cluttered desk. Unfortunately, after what happened recently on top of my "creative" desk, I can make no such claim. It was the day we were booked to see Dickens' *Christmas Carol* at the Geary Theater in San Francisco. We were to meet a relative with whom we were to share the holiday performance. A few minutes before departure time, I rummaged around my desk looking for the tickets, which I knew were there. A confident, leisurely search quickly turned into a frantic one, as my hands stirred the dusty, faded clippings, notices from the bank, unopened letters from the Red Cross, or photos from long ago graduations, but failed to find the precious pieces of cardboard.

It was time to go, but there were no tickets and no time left to sift through the archaeological layers that the search had disturbed. Inescapable was the irony of the predicament that a "creative" mess was blocking the chance to see one of the most creative works of art on the stage. Even though several weeks remained in the current year, an eavesdropper would have heard earnest, even fervent New Year's resolutions voiced on the subject of desk top reform. Words of contrition and vows of change continued throughout the trip to San Francisco.

The desperate plan of last resort was to throw myself on the mercy of the box office staff with the most convincing drama we could muster, hoping that a little theater would not go unappreciated at the Geary.

Consequently, upon arrival, my wife summoned forth her best Tiny Tim impression, and I rummaged around in my facial closet to find the mask of a straight arrow, honest Abe, or more appropriately, an earnest Bob Cratchit countenance, meanwhile training my Scrouge Suppressant mobile device (patent pending) on the inscrutable face behind the ticket window, in the hope that some spirit of holiday forgiveness might prevail after hearing our tale of woe. Our guest, my sister Martha, waited anxiously in the wings for the outcome of the drama. Judging by the size of the eager throng outside the theater, this was apt to be a sold-out performance, so last-minute ticket adjustments might be impossible.

Inside the ticket window, the clerk gave no hint at first of the effect of our drama, but eventually she emerged from the office and, smilingly, handed me three tickets, replacing the missing ones with the wish that we enjoy the show. We recognized her then as the familiar head usher, and she had already recognized us as long-time attendees. As our anxiety melted away, so did my earlier passionate promises about tidying my unruly desk; my creative desk could remain safe for now from pre-New Year's resolutions.

January 2014

My Other Self

It sometimes requires all my energy to keep that forbidden self securely bottled up. Eternal vigilance is the price of keeping my phantom contained, in order to maintain some semblance of psychic integrity and sanity. I have used every tool and strategy I can think of to keep him at a safe distance, but there are times when he rears his multi-horned head with puffy cheeks and saliva dripping between his fangs, tormenting me and creating mischief in my life.

Slava, that is the name I call him, not only thrives, but subsists wholly on one substance: pastry. A faint odor of baking tarts or cinnamon rolls can arouse him from deepest lethargy to feverish agitation, taking over possession of my nervous system and causing my feet to turn upwind to track down the source of that forbidden substance. If I am driving, I have to avoid streets where there are bakeries if I don't want to lose control of the steering wheel to Slava.

Slava will, on certain days, pull the drapes, and in privacy, watch his favorite TV program, *The Great British Baking Show.* It is for him the equivalent of pornography, but he is housebroken enough that he keeps at hand a towel to sop up the copious saliva that comes dripping from his open mouth as he leers at the glazed pastries with raisins and pecans peeking through their thin veil of crust. His envy of the tasters who judge that baking competition is so obvious, I think that if it weren't for some serious security difficulties at the airport that he is apt to encounter, he might well be jetting off to the British Isles and leaving me in peace.

Well-meaning friends, when they catch a glimpse of his flabby abdomen and pudgy countenance, have suggested to me various treatment strategies for him, such as PA, that is, Pastries Anonymous, or some secluded rural residential treatment center for those with alcohol or drug problems. But Slava always maintains that he doesn't have an addiction problem. It's more like a supply problem. If he only had reliable, ready access to pastry, he claims, trying to convince me to be more relaxed about it, he wouldn't have to scheme so much

to get it or to binge so much. As supporting evidence, he points to
the growing legalization of marijuana. He tries to persuade me that if
I would only try some myself, I might open my eyes to be more
understanding and less critical. But I know that down that sinful road
lies the madness of indulgence and obesity, so it seems I am doomed
forevermore to be dogged by Slava, my inner self.

July 2017

A Glance in the Mirror

A visit with our great-granddaughter Rowan, age ten months, was a welcome treat; her cute features and pleasure in exploring new faces, such as our own, absorbed our attention. However, it was also an experience that caused some reflective moments for me. She had recently taken her first steps unaided, and was tottering around from chair leg to table leg, then falling down on her behind. This behavior reminded me, with some discomfort, of my own stage of development. I must look like I am three sheets to the wind sometimes, especially when I am walking outside in the garden, just stepping over a crack in the walkway or over the garden hose. Insignificant objects can be serious challenges to my vertical orientation; I struggle with the law of gravity.

Why won't our legislators in Washington heed my appeals to repeal the law of gravity for seniors? Probably they are beholden to the cane and crutch lobby. Where is the American Association of Retired Persons (AARP) on this issue?

So, is this what they mean by second childhood? An example of both stages were at that moment in the same room together. However, there are some differences. For example, First Child has a shock-absorbing cushion on her derriere, serving double purpose as a diaper, whereas my shock insulation is mere flesh and bone. Maybe there is more than one good reason for Second Childhood persons to wear adult diapers.

Another difference is that two parents stand ready to rescue her when she stumbles over something, in contrast to my predicaments when I have to grab at whatever is handy. if I can reach something, like a bush or tree branch if I don't have my walking stick.

So, there may be lessons to be learned for a Second Childhood person from observing the First.

September 10, 2019

BOB WILKINSON

An Uncommon Occupation

On a recent evening TV program that I occasionally watch, usually only half-heartedly, my attention was drawn to the listed occupations of the participants. One was a business consultant, another a deputy district attorney; the third was indicated as an octogenarian and accordionist. At first, the thought crossed my mind that octogenarian must be a scientific designation for someone who studies that eight-armed creature, the octopus, before realizing its true meaning. It was unstated which was his day job, but I am assuming it was as octogenarian because I know how that stage in life can require nearly full-time attention and effort to maintain. Although I have survived that decade, I still have some unresolved issues with it, now that I realize that what I lived through was apparently listable as an occupation.

If a census taker were to knock on his door, going down the list of questions on the regulation form, there would certainly be that of occupation. "Are you retired, sir?"

His response might well be, "No, I am a stay-at-home octogenarian."

Now, if through no fault of his own, he did not make it to the end of that decade, while he is presumably exchanging his accordion for a harp, will he be wondering if his survivors will be entitled to his unemployment benefits?

It is unclear what would happen if, instead of being laid off, he were demoted. Does that mean that he would get to live the eighties all over again? That could be appealing, because one could re-enter the octogenarian decade again after the earlier apprenticeship, a bit wiser the second time around.

Any offer by his boss of promotion would, I assume, be instantly declined, if that means being bumped up into one's nineties earlier than expected.

Now, having graduated from the octogenarian decade myself, I can attest to the reasonableness of someone claiming it as an occupation. First, the task of finding one's car in the parking lot requires more time and patient detective work than one is usually given credit for. At the least, it requires a lengthy slog through ten acres of cars, searching for that familiar sign, the ding and scrape on the rear fender. There can be no more pitying scene than that of an older man leaving a supermarket exit and coming to a standstill, his eyes betraying bewilderment as he scans the parking lot, while he tries to recall where he last parked, his arms sagging under the weight of a gallon of milk, perhaps a young grandchild tugging at his hand. However, technology may be coming to his rescue with driverless cars; with merely a tap on a hand-held device, the autonomous car will start up and come dashing to his side like an affectionate puppy, his tail wagging and waiting to be petted on the head.

At home, there is the energy spent in trying to recall the reason for going to the refrigerator and opening its door. Was it to fetch the ketchup? If so, whatever for? Was it the yogurt? The vegetable oil? In a devil-may-care spirit, I have selected the sour cream, which when added to the soup, isn't bad.

One's brain can expend only so much effort without exhausting its reservoir of energy, so trying to recall the name of a friend of decades, or of a cousin known for a lifetime, can become a taxing, dispiriting, all-day job. To win a passing grade in the class of Octogenarianism 101, a student could fall back on the family photo album solution, searching through hundreds of photos to see if a name can be connected to a picture.

Then there is that nearly full-time chore requiring one's complete cognitive alertness: the battle with that nemesis of the octogenarian, the law of gravity. Congress has so far remained tone deaf to every petition to repeal it for seniors. I am sure a couple of investigative journalists could uncover the so-far hidden congressional scandal of how senators and representatives are lobbied and financially rewarded by the medical establishment to keep the law in place, particularly those who profit from the application of casts on arms and legs, and the companies that sell canes and hip replacements. A Pulitzer Prize awaits their headline-making story. However, modern entrepreneurship may divert attention from the initiative. Elon Musk, the founder of SpaceX, predicts that the company will send colonists to the moon within a decade. Because the force of gravity is weaker there, I expect to be at the head of the line of applicants.

December 2017

Lost

Opening the front door that morning, I was greeted by a chill, the sun managing only a faint blush on the cheek of the horizon. I stepped bravely out for my usual early morning walk. Unlike other hardy souls I was likely to meet, I was accompanied, not by a dog on leash, but only by my trusty walking stick and the comforting presence of a muffler about my neck. I had tramped only about two hundred yards up the street on my usual path, with no traffic to be mindful of, when I noticed a patrol car rounding the curve, coming in my direction. It was a little surprising to see police in our quiet neighborhood so early in the day. I moved a little closer to the edge of the street to give the vehicle plenty of room to pass. To my surprise, the patrol car did not pass, but instead came to an abrupt halt just a few yards ahead, and the policeman got out, stepping purposefully toward me.

Being on foot, I could not imagine what traffic signs I could have missed or the driving errors I could have committed. I was not intoxicated or going about unclothed, so what was up?

The patrolman addressed me as he approached.

"A lady called us to report that an elderly gentleman was walking on the street and seemed to be lost."

"Elderly gentleman, lost you say? I haven't seen anyone like that since I have been walking," I replied. He looked me over a moment longer, then murmured something and returned to his vehicle, speeding off.

As I resumed my walk, the possible import of what had just happened began to percolate in my mind. Was he thinking I might be that person the caller had been concerned about? Do I look like an elderly gentleman? What on earth could give the patrolman that idea? Well, aside from the negligible matter of being in my nineties, what could it be? Do I appear lost? As though to put an end to that notion, I quickened my pace even though it was an uphill effort. I straightened up and arranged my facial expression so that I would not appear absent minded, but determined, and alert to my surroundings.

Well, perhaps there are signs of being lost. Was I not feeling that way only the day before when my grandson was trying to teach me the intricacies of the new laptop he had so generously given us? I even had to be told how to turn it on, to say nothing about its other mysteries. It takes very little in this digital age for me to feel lost. Maybe it shows on my face the next day—a new wrinkle or two, or something akin to the thousand-yard stare of someone who has been through much trauma. Or maybe it's the gradual corrosive effect on body tissues, caused by the unrelenting assault of horrors from Washington, that seem to come from some lost continent. As a remedy, I should probably stick to just reading the sports pages.

Grudgingly, I could feel a growing respect for that policeman's power of observation.

February 2018

My Many-Faced Monster

Although my worst demon is a shape-shifter, capable of assuming various intimidating forms, its most common appearance is as an apparition with no eyes, no mouth, or nose. It has no legs or tail, no fur or scales, but two unequal-sized arms with twelve digits. It is apt to pop up in most any place to confront me with accusations, despite my most strenuous efforts to ignore it. Another shape it all too often takes is that of four-and-a-half horizontal rows of numbers hanging on the kitchen wall, often with a disarming photo, such as of polar bear cubs, framed above, as though to distract me from its unrelenting and sinister progress. It is futile to try to obscure it, such as to turn it against the wall. Its silent, voracious appetite for life's most precious commodity continues undeterred, no matter what offering I make to try to placate it, or efforts to get ahead of it, such as by getting up earlier in the morning. It only takes revenge by putting me asleep in the afternoon.

An ancient Chinese proverb says that an inch of gold will not buy one inch of it. Chaucer said that it fleets, and will not abide. To quote Omar Khayyam, "The bird of time has but a little way to flutter, and the bird is on the wing." So far, the only technological way to counter it, I have been told, is to travel eastward at the speed of light, although one would need an atomic clock to prove it.

We all discovered recently how the monster can cheat us of an hour; timepieces everywhere conspired together to accomplish the thievery. To say that they will return the hour to us in the fall is but cold comfort—we all may be beyond caring by then.

If a grandchild with a seeming eternity ahead should wonder what is so important about it, why so much agony over a few lost hours or days, aren't there plenty left? What do you need the time for? I would say to myself:

Why, for another cup of coffee and to watch the telly,
stretch and yawn and scratch my belly.

BOB WILKINSON

Give me more time and something will surface,
I'm sure I'll find something to give my hours purpose.

But, in obsessing about my monster, I might only be exemplifying
what La Bruyere, a 17th century French moralist, meant when he
observed that "those who make the worst use of time most complain
of its shortness." I had better overcome my fear of the time monster
if I am to avoid unnecessarily acting like I am long in the tooth.
Otherwise, I might come to resemble what Thoreau, who, probably
in ill-informed youthfulness, wrote: "How earthy old people
become…They remind me of earthworms."

March 2018

The Senses: A Visual Disorientation

Eighteen-wheeled trucks emblazoned with Safeway, or Walmart, breezed past us on the unfamiliar highway. "Where are the logging and lumber trucks?" I mumbled under my breath, "and the smoky saw mills?" Nondescript buildings, motel, and gas station signs slip past. No cows? Where is Highway 99? Gone, along with Orange Julius stands.

Nothing that greets my eyes matches the mental template recalled from long ago. Can this be the place where we spent six impressionable years and where every neighborhood and street corner was familiar? A population sign posted on the highway claims an unimagined figure. The sight of a motel name hoisted on top of a high steel post near an exit from the highway signals a destination which matches our written notes, but not our disbelieving eyes. However, like aviators flying blind in black storm clouds, trained to rely on the instrument panel, we turned to a letter of instructions sent from an old friend to find our auto-landing pad in the gathering mists and darkness. Glad to arrive, but disappointed by our confusion and sense of alienation, we tried to restore our inner balance over dinner and conversation with our old friend, whose residence in the community spanned at least six decades.

"You remember the Johnsons?" my wife inquired, recalling a name from years past.

"She died of breast cancer several years ago," replied our friend.

"And her husband?" I asked.

"He passed away long before she did," was the reply.

"And the lumber mill that he managed?" I said as recollections trickled back.

BOB WILKINSON

"Closed years ago," was the response, with an intonation and glance from her well-lined face that suggested negligence on our part for not keeping in better touch. And so it went.

The next morning's attempts at a visual reorientation began with the reassuring sight of a familiar peak shining in the distance, its perpetual cloak of snow brilliant in the morning sun. This at least was a constant and enduring polar star. In the middle distance a bend in the river could be glimpsed, its dull aluminum-like sheen reflecting in the early morning light.

Tracing the multi-creased map with our fingers, we sought the location of a remembered landmark—an elementary school where my wife taught, and in our recollection, a rural location across the river on a meandering country lane surrounded by green pasture and the occasional rustic farm house. The sight of an ugly brown warehouse dominating a typical discount shopping district greeted us instead. Where was the bucolic country school, the center of communal life in that small town? Were we seeking a will of the wisp Norman Rockwell tableau that never existed except in nostalgic sepia-toned archives of memory? Just then, sandwiched between a Burger King and a retail shop stood the school, or at least the sign proclaimed, "Meadow Lane School," despite any sign of a meadow.

Moving on to find the church whose fifty-year reunion was the primary occasion of our journey, we again followed written instructions, directions which flew in the face of all our remembered sense of place. We joined fast-moving traffic on a boulevard where no road had existed, passing a residential section of modern, prosperous looking homes where manzanita and oak once stretched out into the distance. No sign of the modest Depression-era-like homes we once knew and lived in.

Having at last arrived, we studied the unfamiliar Frank Lloyd Wright building, partially dug into the gently-sloping, shrub-clothed hillside. Inside, the ambience was enlivened by a cheerful kaleidoscope of colors from the bright sunlight, penetrating a series of triangular windows set along the corner formed by the eastern wall and the natural wooden beamed ceiling. Among the pleasant, murmuring hubbub were smiling gray- and snowy-haired women, who formed a friendly greeting party bestowing red-framed name tags on visitors, the only clue we bewildered members of the church diaspora might have for visual recognition of friends and acquaintances from half a century ago.

Where were some men that I might remember? Dead? Divorced? Departed? None I knew were in sight, until the minister of long ago, recalled from a distant retirement community, appeared at the pulpit to add at least a symbolic nod to the senior gender balance.

So, this is the modern city that has taken the place of the town we remembered. Its malls, museum, two structures by world famous architects—no longer the provincial community where once efforts had been made by elected leaders to close the public library because in the immortal words of one, "Television is available now, and the local drug store has books you can buy."

This is the town where elementary school teachers worked double jobs such as a small dairy keeper or manager of a root beer stand to keep the family afloat, where pediatrics and psychiatry specialties were late to arrive, where the only significant racial minority had been American Indians: Wintu, Pit River, etc. They existed mostly out of sight on the fringes of society, but now presumably at least included Latino restaurant workers and motel maids. Today, an urban-like community march to protest inaction for Darfur victims was greeted with no special surprise although uncertain response.

The noisy, dusty, intimidating logging trucks, trailing bark fragments and gray plumes of diesel smoke, what had taken their place? Where were the men I once knew? The questions begged another more fundamental, but unspoken series of questions amounting to "Why had it taken so long for me to return or to inquire?"

January 2007

BOB WILKINSON

The Inheritance

My grandson's inheritance will likely be an old, battered suitcase containing a repair kit equipped to correct for errors in home projects built in his eventual garage workshop. I expect him to become more skilled at building things than I, judging by his fascination with LEGOs, and after all, according to the New Zealand scholar James Flynn, each generation is smarter than the preceding one. Still, he might just have an occasional need for adjusting for unforeseen mistakes, like failure to measure correctly before cutting with the saw.

The first item will be a package of small wood shims. These will be helpful in correcting for errors in the construction of a table or a wobbly chair with mismatched legs. Is the washing machine off balance? No problem; just shove a shim under one leg.

An important second item in the kit will be a roll of duct tape, a tool which binds up many a wounded appliance or leaky pipe which, although common sense says should be replaced, can be done tomorrow, mañana.

The third tool will be a roll of wire. What sins cannot be corrected with wire wound around the offending parts?

There will be one tool to be used for tackling problems unresponsive to duct tape and too big for one person; that would be a pen. It should be used to write his congressperson or state representative urging legislation to correct serious societal problems. For example, he could demand Congress repeal one very outmoded law. That would be the law of gravity for seniors; you can't fix broken hips with a roll of bailing wire. The resulting savings in money would by itself solve the country's debt problems. Successful lobbying for repeal would doubtless require that I include in the kit some length of molding to fashion frames for displaying awards from the MacArthur Foundation or a grateful AARP. He might, however, have to take defensive measures to protect himself from the wrath of the hip replacement industry, so included in the kit will be a disguise package with a false moustache. What more could a grandfather bequeath his young grandson?

December 2012

BOB WILKINSON

The Closet

Rolling up the top of my mother's antique walnut secretary is like opening an old, cobwebby closet or door to a dusty attic. It sets loose a familiar odor of ancient mouse habitation, whether of dead mouse or mouse feces, I'm not quite sure. A thorough search has failed to reveal either; only an olfactory essence remains as an aid to memory. My mother's relationship with the species *mus musculus* was not a cordial one. I was often enlisted to set traps for them, and to empty out any successfully baited victims.

In my childhood our leaky houses must have been as unfortified against rodents as they were against the weather - it was open borders for four footed immigrants. Later on, when we raised chickens, the coop was like a beacon for larger rodents—rats—which not only raided the containers of chicken feed, but also killed the chickens sometimes. They apparently were omnivorous. I assumed the duties of border guard against those greedy critters, using as firepower only my armory of bow and arrows, achieving notoriety for succeeding to some degree, but not quite the nimrod or pied piper that was needed. That might have been the case if I had owned a coveted BB gun. Firearms or BB guns were permitted in my mother's house, but I probably derived more satisfaction in the long run from using archery equipment that I had made myself.

But to get back to my mother's secretary, it contains her memoir hardbound in blue, typed first on her sturdy Underwood, then later, when they became available, on an electric typewriter which was as unfamiliar to me as computers later on. She would probably have taken to using a computer for typing much easier than I did, had she lived a little longer.

In her introduction, she forswears writing about her grandparents, saying that much has already been written. True, but I would have been interested in her recollections, anyway, because they would have been from her unique perspective. For that I can turn to another volume in her secretary, stories written by my grandfather about his

163

childhood, growing up in pioneer 1860's Utah, recalling his experience with his father's demands on him, which would seem questionable to us now in the 21st century. For example, he writes of having to drive a team of horses and wagon at age twelve many miles into the desert to deliver barrels of water to a pair of sun-baked desert rats who were digging a well, on the way encountering mischievous Indians who emptied the barrels into the sand, forcing him to turn back, and at his father's insistence, trying again, alone. Alongside that story, my chores that I complained about as a child pale by comparison.

My grandfather chose not to write about his father's multiple families, which would be of at least as much interest to us, now that they have long been outlawed. With Mother's grandfather's numerous wives, I have sometimes run into relatives that I had no idea existed. And then there came the news during the presidential election of 2012 that I am related to Mitt Romney, because he is descended from my great grandfather's brother. I did not find that to be a very good incentive to study my genealogy. Maybe I would find out that relatives were complicit in the infamous Meadow Mountain Massacre perpetrated by fanatic Mormons disguised as Indians killing non-Mormon immigrants.

I digress. Returning to my mother's secretary, I rediscovered a faded first edition of the Deseret News, the first newspaper printed in Utah, dated June 15, 1850, with the fresh front page news that a fire had all but destroyed San Francisco in the previous December, all of six months earlier. News must have traveled by Turtle Express in those pre-electronic days.

On the back page is the paper's sole advertisement, by a local blacksmith, offering immigrants to have their oxen and horses shod on short notice and "on reasonable terms." There is no mention of offering a fourth horse shod for free or whether Mastercard would be accepted.

BOB WILKINSON

I was about to close the roll top of the secretary when I caught sight of another document from the secretary—an 1876 certificate attesting that my mother's mother had graduated from the "Normal Department" of the University of Deseret, later to become the University of Utah. She was the first woman in the Territory of Utah to do so, according to my mother. Along with it is a Teacher's Certificate authorizing her to teach in the "Common Schools" of Salt Lake City, attesting to her proficiency in both "Mental Arithmetic," as well as "Orthography," a word I had to look up in the dictionary to find out that it means spelling. I try to imagine children competing today for prizes in a televised "Orthography" Bee.

It seems remarkable that my grandmother could have managed, or even aspired to, higher education, after the events in her childhood. Her mother—my mother's grandmother—perished in a snowstorm which nearly killed the children also. My eight-year-old grandmother was left to raise her younger brothers, only to have them die as teenagers, one in a snow avalanche, the other by falling into a Nevada hot springs. Life was not easy in those days, especially if your father also deserts the children to live with his other wives and children.

Here in the secretary I find my mother's recollections about her oldest sister, Dora. I learned as a child to regard my Aunt Dora with almost holy admiration, reflecting my mother's bonds of affection for her. My mother was the youngest of ten children. Dora, the oldest, apparently assumed the role of deputy mother, even supporting the family financially as an associate professor at the University following the disability of their father.

Dora seemed to me, on those few occasions when she visited us here in California, to be a very dignified, almost unapproachable, elderly aunt, always dressed in conservative black or grey, wearing an equally severe-looking hat with veil. Regardless of our distance in age and status, she understood my reading interests, which she sustained by regularly sending me books of adventure, like the tales of Robin Hood, always at my level of reading comprehension and readiness. Thinking of her as an elderly person in those days of childhood when she was only in her mid-fifties, I am shocked now to read in my mother's memoirs that when she died, she was only 66; death at that age now seems to me to be so unfair. I also wonder that, if at fifty-five, she seemed old to me, how impossibly ancient I must seem now to my own young grandchildren.

I had better roll down the top of my mother's secretary before I am accused of running off at the mouth, but before I do, I should mention what was probably the last record of my mother's writing. She wrote:

> Once a year or so everyone should hold a baby. It gives one a completely new look at humanity. One goes about for days feeling tender and kindly toward everyone, for, one realizes, everyone was once a baby...To care for a baby is to find oneself, in the deepest sense, all nervousness washed away, all fussiness, and worry, all that is depressing, all wrong values, all personal concerns rubbed out, and in their place peace and serenity and love.

Those sentiments were written from her long perspective of grandparenthood and of ninety years of living. I'm not sure whether she could have written those sentiments as the young mother of a colicky baby during the Depression years, when there was no money for a doctor and my father was unable to find work.

Now it is high time to close up the secretary with its lingering fragrance of mouse.

February 2014

BOB WILKINSON

Shock

Once, my widowed mother, who by then was in her late eighties, asked me what Dad and I had talked about the time approximately a year before, when he and I had gone into his room together. It was at their retirement home in Walnut Creek in the late 1970's. My father had pulled me aside into his room and shut the door. There, by the bed, was his breathing machine, necessary because of his lung problems. In a very confidential voice, presumably so as not to be overheard by my mother in the next room, he said he wanted me to help him end his life. Although I knew he had been ill for quite some time, and Blossom and I had even tried to help him by bringing in someone schooled in Asian medicine when more conventional medical help hadn't helped, I never knew just how difficult it was for him. So this question took me by complete surprise. More than that, I was shocked. He was about seventy-five years old at this time. Looking back from my present age of ninety-two, it seems now, as it did then, much too young to come to the end of life. But more than that, the concept of someone close to you wanting to die, and further, to be asked to assist him in doing so, was at that time especially incomprehensible.

Now, with the advent of the "Death with Dignity" movement and legislation, it is far less shocking, and I can accept it if someone with terminal illness wished to end his suffering. In fact, later, a minister with whom I was acquainted, worked to have legislation to this end passed in Sacramento. In support, I wrote a letter describing my father's wishes. A friend who is a marriage and family counselor recently told me she has written a book about it in response to requests she has received in her counseling sessions. Another acquaintance whose girlfriend had been terminally ill apparently assisted in her death, not by taking a "death pill" or doctor-assisted injection, but by refusing nourishment. However, something I can accept intellectually is different from an emotional acceptance when it involves someone close to you.

I'm not sure what my mother thought when I shared my father's request with her after the fact, or of my response to decline to assist him. By that time, it was only a footnote perhaps, but nevertheless further evidence of his suffering and our inability to adequately help him.

June 2019

BOB WILKINSON

Bellytimber in Community

Senior Living?

Senior living is fine for elder citizens who are unable to care for themselves, I said to our children. When I get to that age, I will certainly give it some thought. Here are some of my reactions to what I have seen on my senior living visits:

1. Walkers: Most people have to use them, but I don't. Well, OK, I guess you have a point. I am holding onto Blossom's wheelchair.

2. I'm not as old looking as they are! Oh! That mirror! It lies; it's probably damaged.

3. They supply drivers for appointments and do the shopping that residents may need? You mean give up driving? Nonsense! What's that, you say? The yellow paint smudge on the fender of the car? I have no idea how that got there. I realize that it may be the same color as the concrete pillar in the garage next to the car, but maybe someone spilled paint there.

4. Meals are provided? But I can cook. They serve ambrosia salad and mulligatawny soup? You can order a glass of wine at meal time? And no dishes to wash? I'll have to think about it.

5. Doughnuts are served to us in our apartments twice a week? Why didn't you say so? Pastry is one of my anchors in a life of uncertainties.

6. Although it may not be mentioned as a premier advantage, it's hard not to notice that the mortuary is just across the street.

7. How did our adult children become so wise?

June 2021

BOB WILKINSON

Bellytimber Talk

Recently, I ran across a book about old English with a listing of some words no longer in use. Of course, the story of our language is one of new words being incorporated almost daily, but I wonder if our language would be even richer if we didn't lose so many really choice expressions. I must have been so affected by how much we have lost, that I dreamed of encountering two of my ancient, long-forgotten cousins from 16th Century England. Afterward, I awoke to quickly jot down the conversation before I could forget it. We had met on our way to dinner. Here is the gist of it:

"Hurry up," the first cousin Michael said, "We don't want to be *sloomy* and have to kiss the hare's foot; I can't wait for my evening merry-go-down." (be lazy and late for our meal, with ale)

The second cousin Edward said, "Let's not *squiddle* any longer." (waste time with idle talk) "I could sure use some *hum* and good *bellytimber*." (strong liquor and food)

Michael said, "The last time we ate at that inn you were so *mubblefubbled* you hardly even *pingled*." (depressed and ate very little)

"That's because there was so much noisy *whoopubb*. (hubbub) "But now, my *pash* fairly *quops*." (forehead throbs) "I am going to tell that *hoddynoddy* of a *nickpot*" (stupid blockhead of an innkeeper) "that I want to have some real tipsycake," (cake soaked in wine) "not that *maw-wallop* he served last time. It was like *mung*" (badly cooked like chicken feed), Edward replied.

"Does your *poplollie* (mistress) know you are going to the *reelpot*? (tavern), or is it *hudder-mudder*? (secret) between us?" Michael asked.

"We had some *brangling* and snarky (noisy and nauseating) words about it until I promised to be *hoful* (careful) about the *roverdavy* (wine)," Edward replied. "But she wouldn't let me have more than

171

just a little *chinkers* (money). However, that didn't cause me any *mentmutation* (change of mind)."

The *welkin* (evening sky) showed that it was getting late, so the cousins walked off to have their *bellytimber* (food).

March 2018

BOB WILKINSON

Those Brilliant Red Plants

Have you ever seen such red,
Where green should be instead?

Those blazing lights across our retinas
Are attention-grabbing poinsettias.

Perhaps the glow is stolen from the sun,
Ever wondered where old sol goes when day is done?

To hold them in steady gaze you lads and lasses,
You must put on summer dark glasses.

Might they be a beacon to steer
Season's Santa and reindeer?

December 2021

In the Sterling Court Dining Room

As each resident folds into a chair
disengages from walker and settles with care,

Smile as they expectantly lift off their mask,
scrutinize the menu, choices are the next task.

The waiter appears quickly at their table
to solicit their wishes as soon as they are able.

Helping them with the menu if they can't see,
asparagus, potato, or green pea.

Then, friskily to the kitchen the orders to fill,
whether fried, baked, or from the grill.

Stepping forth, she is confident, graceful in stride,
no hesitation, limping, or leaning to one side.

Then, out of the kitchen bursts the waiter with tray, soup bowls on top,
agile, balletic, spilling not a drop.

When the diner is ready to leave
they remember which walker to retrieve.

Such energy, dexterous ability,
their motion conveys serene tranquility.

As I watch in envy their energetic motion
I can't help but be struck by this notion:

Is there wisdom in serving us old fossils;
will they absorb through their pores or nostrils

BOB WILKINSON

Enough old folks' virus to gain immunity
from eventual senescence, arthritis, and senility?

If not based on science, biologically,
might it at least be so psychologically?

Or, in reverse, as we see their ambulation, perhaps,
at least we can imagine emulation.

SEPIA-TONED ARCHIVES

Three Pines

Three pines standing silent, steps from the door,
Offer greetings, stability, and lore.
A visit from a bird—the Brown Creeper—hunting in bark crevices
For the furtive spider or bug,
Does it itch or tickle? The pine gives not a shrug.

Plumber's truck arriving to clear a clogged drain,
The pines, indifferent, felt no pain.
To honor resident's 95th birthday, son and son
bring bright balloons,
But no whisper from the pines of any celebratory tunes.

Spring winds may blow, rocking shrubs and flowers to and fro,
But the sentinel pines with unmovable spines,
Regardless of buffets, taunts, or malice.
Remain unperturbed like guards at Buckingham Palace.

The young crow from shelter in the pines descends to the street
Unfamiliar with objects he may meet,
Is struck by a truck from the rear,
The pines—no shedding of needle or tear.

Ambulance arriving with siren and red light,
From the pines—no wilting at stroke patient's sudden plight.

Its nemesis, the tree cutting truck with wood grinder behind,
The pines do not tremble, paying it no mind.

Ol' Sol's temp in June, summer heat coming soon,
Pine's casting welcome shade,
better than any umbrella made.
They care less than two hoots,
As long as water gets to their roots.

BOB WILKINSON

The trunks, sturdy, stretching high to better know
The life in upper regions rather than what passes below.
Perhaps the pines being an aloof patient sort,
Envision the building named for them in the future
Instead of Sterling Court.

SEPIA-TONED ARCHIVES

About the Author

Bob Wilkinson was born in 1926, after his mother, already in labor, rode the street car by herself from San Mateo to San Francisco to give birth in a hospital. He spent his childhood in Southern California and the Montclair hills of Oakland, where his family survived the Great Depression with limited resources. Shortly after the end of World War II, Bob was drafted into the military at age nineteen. In 1951, he married elementary school teacher May-Blossom Chang Wilkinson. Bob earned a Masters in Social Work from the University of California at Berkeley, and was the intake unit supervisor of Children's Protective Services in San Mateo County.

In middle-age, Bob focused his efforts on anti-war protest, environmental activism, and public art advocacy. In retirement, Bob maintained a dedicated art practice carving wood sculpture, and sharing his talents in artists' open studio events in Belmont and Burlingame over the years. A life-long nature enthusiast and voracious reader, Bob has a keen eye for observation. He wrote many of the pieces in this book while attending memoir writing classes at the San Mateo Senior Center and the Foster City Senior Center, and wishes to acknowledge instructor Katherine Lieban, who inspired him. His artistic pursuits have included a penchant for poetry, humorous anecdotes, and compelling short stories that recount moments of joy and curiosity about the world around him. A dedicated family man, Bob has four children, seven grandchildren, and one great-grandchild. He lives in San Mateo, California.

SEPIA-TONED ARCHIVES

Made in the USA
Middletown, DE
07 November 2023

41950177R00109